The Crowning of Louis

The Crowning of Louis

A New Metrical Translation of the Old French Verse Epic

edited and translated by
Nirmal Dass

McFarland & Company, Inc., Publishers
Jefferson, North Carolina, and London

Library of Congress Cataloguing-in-Publication Data

Couronnement de Louis. English & French (Old French)
    The crowning of Louis : a new metrical translation of the old French verse epic / edited and translated by Nirmal Dass.
       p.   cm.
    Includes index.
    ISBN 0-7864-1560-6 (softcover: 50# alkaline paper)
    1. Louis I, Emperor, 778–840 — Romances.   I. Dass, Nirmal, 1962–
II. Title.
PQ1453.C6E5   2003
841'.1— dc21   2002156434

British Library cataloguing data are available

©2003 Nirmal Dass. All rights reserved

No part of this book may be reproduced or transmitted in any form or by any means, electronic or mechanical, including photocopying or recording, or by any information storage and retrieval system, without permission in writing from the publisher.

Cover art: Pope Hadrian I crowns Louis the Pious as Charlemagne looks on in 781 A.D. BNF, FR 2813, fol. 128, *Grandes Chroniques de France,* Paris, 14th century illuminated manuscript, 60 × 65 mm (*Bibliothèque nationale de France/Gallica*)

Manufactured in the United States of America

McFarland & Company, Inc., Publishers
  Box 611, Jefferson, North Carolina 28640
    www.mcfarlandpub.com

urit grata protervitas
et vultus nimium lubricus aspici.

Table of Contents

Introduction	1
The Crowning of Louis	15
Notes to the Translation	86
Glossary	101
Bibliography	115
Index	117

Introduction

The Crowning of Louis is an anonymous work dating from about 1130–1140. Linguistic evidence suggests that it was composed in northern France, more specifically in the regions of Picardy or Ile-de-France.[1] This epic has come down to us in nine manuscripts, the majority of which date from the thirteenth century.[2]

Typical of heroic poetry of the time (the *chanson de geste*), *The Crowning* is divided into *laisses* or stanzas, of which there are sixty-three, of varying lengths, each distinguished by a single rhyme or assonance. Each line has ten syllables and is marked by a pause (or caesura).

Epics such as *The Crowning* were typically performance pieces, sung or chanted by minstrels (*jongleurs*)[3] at special gatherings. The chanting was accompanied by an early type of viol (*vieille*), and there was likely a musical interlude after each *laisse* was sung and before the next one began.[4] Performance implies orality, and it is not surprising to find in *The Crowning* features peculiar to oral literature, such as stock phrases and formulaic episodes. As well, the performer (the "I") often interjects the self in order to hold forth or pass judgment. Further, the persona of the performer gives *The Crowning* its motivational force in that the entire piece is being sung for a reward. This pragmatic approach mirrors the driving force behind the execution of valorous deeds by William, the hero of *The Crowning*: William's actions hinge upon the notion of reward, either material (land, money, or titles), or abstract (honor, praise, or salvation). The oral nature of *The Crowning* is further highlighted by the claim that the recital of the epic took several days and nights (ll. 313–314); this is certainly plausible given the length of the poem.[5]

Epics were popular presentations, often held in conjunction with other forms of entertainment. They would be sung at fairs, in town squares, or in the halls of local lords or barons. These epics recounted the deeds of famous heroes, stressing their marvelous exploits, their piety and strength, and their loyalty and honor. For the medieval world, history was a series of events from which one could draw moral lessons. There was very little concern for historical accuracy as we understand it.

During the time when *The Crowning* was being performed and came to be written down, France was in the middle of an exuberantly creative period now termed the twelfth century Renaissance. Two kings ruled during this period: Louis VI, also known as Louis the Fat, and his son Louis VII. Paris was the center of their royal power. In architecture, the soaring and airy Gothic style began to replace the somber and heavy Romanesque. Cities such as Amiens, Beauvais, Rheims, Rouen and Chartres were growing fast, producing an increasingly well-to-do middle class and replacing the influence of manor and abbey. During this time, construction began on the Notre Dame and Abbey Church of St. Denis in Paris and the Cathedral in Chartres. This was the time of stained glass windows, of polyphonic singing, of the two-part and three-part motet, of the first universities in Paris and Chartres; of scholastic philosophy, Gothic dualism, the growth of vernacular literature, aesthetics and number theory. This was the time of men like Thomas Aquinas, Albertus Magnus, Bonaventura, Thomas Becket, and the tragic Peter Abelard.[6] Thus, although *The Crowning* harks back to the Dark Ages, the audience for which it was composed and performed was very much removed from the imperatives of the eighth and ninth centuries. This distinction between the past and the present, myth and reality, is important if we wish to understand something about the nature of the epic in the twelfth century.

Chansons de geste ("songs of heroic deeds," or epics)[7] are commonly divided into three great cycles: the cycle of Charlemagne (which includes the famous *Song of Roland*), the cycle of the rebellious barons, and the cycle of William of Orange, which is the largest group, comprising some twenty-four epics. *The Crowning*, of course, is part of the cycle of William of Orange.

But how are we to understand the nature of the Old French epic? In order to answer this question, we must first ask: What is the nature of history in the medieval age? Or rather what is history within the epic? What does it signify? How are we to view the *chanson de geste*? Is it *res gestae* ("the history of things," the totality of events, the unfolding of human civilization), or is it *historia rerum gestarum* ("a narrative of events")?

On the superficial level, we can say that we are dealing with very specific events presented as a cohesive narrative report or account: the deeds of William of Orange, or more precisely his continual defense of royal authority. But the medieval mind would have also seen the *chanson de geste* as *res gestae*, wherein events were uniquely linked with God's will, or perhaps even destiny, for history was that place wherein God's plan for humankind unfolded and revealed itself.

Thus for the medieval mind, history was theocentric, for without God history made no sense; without a divine blueprint, there was only chaos. And the pagans and Saracens we meet in *The Crowning* are part of that chaos, for they exist outside God's order, his blueprint. In fact, they are errant, disruptive forces that need to be assimilated or destroyed. Thus, Corsolt is killed and King Galafrez converted to Christianity. In effect, the *chanson de geste* is a narrativization of a specific past – a past which demonstrates that chaos is God's other; it is the disruptive force by which God's blueprint can be completely derailed. This is the ideology behind Corsolt's boast in Laisse 19 that he chased God away from the earth.

This view of history as the workings of redemption (God's plan) also suggests that God needs heroes, like William, who can undertake the holy task of destroying chaos. We shall elaborate on this valorization of the warrior ethic a little later on.

Also, hidden deep within *The Crowning* are traces of *historia rerum gestarum*, or a narrative of events, fragments of other lives and events to which we can give an objective historical reality as we know it. In effect, *The Crowning* is layered with history.

The title of the work certainly suggests a description of objective reality: The coronation of Louis the Pious (A.D. 778–840), the son and heir of Charlemagne (A.D. 768–814). But is it?

Louis the Pious was crowned at Aix-la-Chapelle in 813, just before the death of his father, Charlemagne. He was thirty-six years of age, and was certainly no child that needed the protection of William of Orange. If we move forward some three hundred years, we learn that in 1131 Louis VI crowned his son, a mere child, as King Louis VII.[8] This sort of crowning was unusual at the time, because kings were traditionally chosen from a group of barons. However, Louis VI wanted to make the French crown hereditary (a project in which he was much aided by Bishop Suger).

Returning to *The Crowning*, we must ask which Louis is the subject of the *chanson*. Given the layering of history, the answer must be both Charlemagne's son *and* Louis VII, because the real subject of *The Crowning* is not the life story of one king, but rather the life of kings, the link between regal authority and divine authorization of regality. Thus, *The Crowning* narrativizes the modes through which kingship is legitimized by providing an example from the past that comments on the contemporary life of twelfth century France. In effect, *The Crowning* is a generalization by way of the particular. Therefore, the *chanson de geste* is *exemplum*; that is, a narrative presented as truthful (historical) in order to edify the listener: Regal authority is divinely ordained and therefore cannot be transgressed. To do so invites divine and social retribution. Thus all the rebellious barons, such as Arnéïs d'Orléans, Richard of Rouen, and Gui of Germany, are severely punished for rebelling against Louis' authority. And all pagans and Saracens that rebel against God's authority are destroyed or converted.

Certainly, *The Crowning* seeks to impose a cohesive force by narrativizing the heroic deeds of the past into a typological unity.[9] Typology proceeds by juxtaposing two or more events or persons, whereby the first signifies itself and the second, while the second likewise signifies itself and the first. This chiasmus is at the very center of the epic: The hero signifies his own strength, while at the same time signifying the world or society that his strength constructs and thereafter preserves.[10]

Further, we need to understand that the epic is not only archaeological (in that it assembles for us the story of past events), it is also teleological (in that it actively seeks to project into the future by way of the present). The implications of this structure are profound. The epic contains an account of heroic deeds. However, the hero and his deeds are the ground upon which future "history" will be built. The hero performs his mighty deeds and routs chaos in order to give way to, and make visible, the potentiality of the future. Thus the heroic act is not only aggrandizement of the heroic self, but is also an attempt at perfecting the future—and for the medieval mind, the future was always perfect, a place of redemption and paradise.

Another closely related idea of history found in the epic is the placing of present-time beside past-time; the interplay of the two is also chiastic. Present-time is degenerative because it has no heroes and contains only shadows of former glory (ll. 31–35). Thus, the epic is a tropological interpretation of the present.[11] It describes by example the perfectibility of the present in the future. The past is a metaphor by which the present may participate in the metonymy of future eventuation of truth, for the trope both makes the past present and presents what will come in the future as a result of the past. In short, the epic witnesses the occurrence of *alétheia*, the unconcealedness, the unhiddenness, the revelation[12] of what is to be—(for the epic) the trope of salvation. The epic is determined by the idea that the present is always already marred—in fact it cannot exist without this marring, otherwise salvation would be meaningless. Thus even though the hero fights to rout chaos and struggles for order, the future for which he performs these actions is not the present of the twelfth century. Rather that future is the *alétheia* of salvation (the perfection of history itself). Thus, when William defends Rome, he is defending not only the physical city but also the eternal city, the New Jerusalem. And William struggles, not only to annihilate chaos, but to create in his actions the ground in which salvation will reveal itself (salvation in its many forms: defeat of the Saracens, crowning of Louis, security of the realm and redemption of the soul). If we extend the trope of salvation, we see that the epic posits the interpreting subject (itself, its author and its audience) as part of the symbolized object (the future perfect). But are we any closer to a definition of an epic?

One way to define the epic is to see it as the prehistory of the novel, as postulated by Mikhail Bakhtin. According to Bakhtin, the epic is primarily an expression of reality (as is the novel), and as such it presents a world that is completed and perfected. Further, this world is far removed from the author and the audience by an inaccessible and remote past. The epic actively seeks to valorize a particular time and thus endorses its closedness, for it speaks of legend, which is sacrosanct and unarguable. An epic is not a reflection of its time, but it is a very particular snapshot of the ideas of a given time and a given society.[13] Thus, the epic seeks to unify and centralize meaning in order to manifest scheme, method and orderliness.

The problem with Bakhtin is that he uses the epic as the other for the novel. He fails to consider that the epic also is a social construction of meaning, and as such (like the novel) is replete with heteroglossia (a term much favored by Bakhtin)—forces that defy unification and centralization. For example, *The Crowning* is not merely about the legitimacy of regal power; it is also a contention of voices, an agon of the centripetal and centrifugal forces of language. We hear the voices of lords and commoners, clergy and laity, Christians and pagans, men, women and children, belief and disbelief, old and young, the past and present, captivity and liberation, the personal and the social, the ethical and the unethical. The contention of difference, the force of heteroglossia, is at play not only in the novel, but also in the epic. This is why Bakhtin's view is inadequate as a definition for the epic.

There is an evolutionary sense in Bakhtin, whereby literature goes through stages in order to arrive at the novel, the perfected stage.[14] The problem with such an evolutionary system is that it is exclusive and perhaps even arrogant—people of the past are seen as children by way of our own modern, grownup, and mature hindsight. But it is important to realize that language is always already complete in itself, at any given time. Likewise, literature is always already complete in itself, at any given time. Literature and language do not evolve (which inherently implies a march towards an as yet unnamed state of perfection), but they do change, and these changes reflect the needs and vicissitudes of the community of speakers of a language or a literature. Thus, the epic does not contain the prehistory of the novel, wherein the novel evolves and perfects itself. Nor is the epic the expression of a childish, benighted society that has yet to grow up. Rather the epic is a linguistic or literary act complete in itself, for it contains the needs of its community of speakers and listeners.

Then how are we to understand the epic? We must see it as a constellation of past and present moments. And within the dialectical image of the constellation (the construction of a past moment within a present one) occur readability, the flash of insight, a brief recognition.[15] The epic exists only as a constellation, where fragmentary elements, bereft of their own context in the past, are placed within the newer context of the present. These fragments from the past no longer have any connection with the time from which they descend; rather they become the objective interpretations of the phenomenal world — for the past is gone forever; all we ever have are fragments which we seek to fashion into a meaningful image, like a jigsaw puzzle from which many pieces will always be missing. And these fragments are meaningful for ourselves, not for those for whom these fragments were complete objects.

If we define the epic as a constellation of fragments of past and present moments, can we discern any such fragments in *The Crowning*?

Immediately, we have the two historical men named Louis: the son of Charlemagne and the son of Louis VI. In other words, a Louis from the past and a Louis contemporary with the epic.

Louis the Pious (or Louis the Debonair), the son of Charlemagne, was born in 778 at Chasseneuil in Bordeaux. He was crowned king at Aix-la-Chapelle in 813, after the death of Charlemagne; he was thirty-six years old at the time. He certainly was not a child, as *The Crowning* tells us. However, he was a weak king, easily overawed by his bishops and his sons.[16] Tradition remembers him as a feeble king, vainly trying to assert his authority — the divine right of kings is an important theme in *The Crowning*.

In 817, Louis decreed he would pass on his empire to his son Lothair I, whom he appointed co-emperor. This broke with Carolingian tradition of equally dividing the realm among all the sons. To his other sons, Pepin I and Louis the German, he gave Aquitaine and Bavaria respectively. However, he soon remarried and had another son, Charles (who later became Emperor of the West as Charles II), for whom he consequently sought to create a realm. This led to open revolt by his older sons. After much strife, Louis managed to put down the revolt, but because of his piety, he agreed to undergo a public penance in 822 at the church of Attigny, in order to expiate his persecution of those involved in the revolt.[17]

In 830, Lothair again rebelled, deposed his father and became sole ruler of the empire. However, his two brothers were not happy to see so much power vested in Lothair. They released their father and restored him to the throne. And yet again another revolt broke out in 833, in which all three sons took part. Louis met the rebels at the Field of Lies (Lügenfeld, near Colmar), so named because there was a general defection of Louis' troops to the rebel cause. Again, Louis surrendered and was deposed, and Lothair became emperor. But a year later, Pepin and Louis the German restored their father, Louis the Pious, as a countermeasure against Lothair. Over the next six years, Louis the Pious divided his empire between Lothair and Charles. Louis died in 840 in Ingelheim, Germany, as he was on his way to meet his rebel sons, who yet again opposed Charles' right to any part of the empire.[18] Thus, Louis the Pious came to be seen as an ineffectual king in tradition and history, a fact preserved in *The Crowning*.

The second Louis who makes up the composite Louis of *The Crowning* is the son of Louis VI, also known as Louis the Fat (1081–1137).

Louis VI was renowned for his prowess in battle and in hunting, and his prodigious appetite was legendary. At the age of forty-six he grew too fat to mount a horse, but he remained energetic. He is best remembered for his success in putting down rogue barons, who behaved little better than robbers. When Louis VI came to the throne, every lord of a castle robbed and pillaged at will; it was not safe even for the king to wander too far from his stronghold. It took Louis twenty years of hard fighting to destroy the robber barons, but in the end, he did bring law and order to the realm.[19] The destruction of rebel barons who oppose the authority of the king is central to *The Crowning*.

In 1131, Louis the Fat crowned his eleven-year-old son as Louis VII (1120–1180), thus ensuring the smooth transition of power. The problem faced by the early Capetians was how to secure the crown for their sons, since kingship was not hereditary but elective (a king was chosen from among the nobels). By crowning his young son, Louis the Fat, with Abbot Suger's support, guaranteed the succession of his young son.[20] Louis the Fat would go on to reign for six more years.[21] Thus, when *The Crowning* speaks of the coronation of the child Louis, the contemporary Louis VII is discernible.

Despite the title of the epic, *The Crowning*'s upholder of regal authority, and by extension of Christianity, is William of Orange. Just as Louis is a mosaic of fragments of two kings named Louis, so William is a collage of many personalities from French history. Let us briefly explore the fragments making up the constellation that is William in *The Crowning*.

The earliest fragment comes from Ermoldus Nigellus, who tells us, in his poem *In honorem Hludovici* ("In Honor of Louis"), that William was a nephew of Charlemagne and a popular hero of his time.[22] He offered to lead an expedition against the Saracens in the south. In support of this claim, we find mentioned in the *Chronicon Moissiacense* for the year 793 that William fought a battle against the Moorish prince Abderraman ibn-Mavia at the River Orbieu.[23]

A fragment from the mid-eleventh century, the *Nota Emilianense*, maintains William's familial link with Charlemagne, telling us that William was one of six nephews of the emperor and accompanied him and the Twelve Peers in the expedition to Sargossa.[24] In the fragment, he is called "Ghilgelmo alcorbitanas," or "William Shortnose" (an epithet maintained in *The Crowning*). There is another text, the Hague Fragment (which is in fact a summary of a Latin poem), that mentions the names of several relatives of William, such as Bertrand and Bernard.[25]

These early accounts all deal with William of Toulouse, with whom Louis the Pious spent a few years as a child in the south of France. Therefore, *The Crowning* places the child and the older warrior together in its narrative structure.

As for William of Toulouse, who later became Saint William, we know he became Duke of Toulouse in 790 and served under the young Louis (who later became Louis the Pious) in Aquitaine, while Charlemagne was still alive. He fought against the Saracens, perhaps in support of Louis. In 804 he founded the abbey of Gellone, under the guidance of Saint Benedict of Aniane; he eventually became a monk at this abbey and died there in 813. Orderic Vitalis (1131–1141)[26] and the *Vita domni Willelmi Abbatis* (ca. 1020)[27] tell us that William won Orange as his realm and that he dealt with King Theodebald, subdued the Saracens, and planted churches throughout southwestern France. When he retired as a monk, he placed his arms at the altar of St. Julian, where they were venerated by pilgrims heading for Santiago de Compostela for many centuries.

Fragments of other lives are also discernible in the jigsaw puzzle. There was William of Montreuil, who led a company of Normans into Spain in 1063 and fought against the Moors. There is William VI and also William IX of Aquitaine, from the early twelfth century, who both battled the Arabs in Spain.[28] It was during the time of these two Williams that *The Crowning* was composed and performed.

Other members of the Aquitaine house can also be mentioned: William I, who founded Cluny and whose mother's name was Ermengard (she is mentioned in *The Crowning*); William Fièrebrace ("Strongarm," the epithet used for William in *The Crowning*), who made pilgrimages to Santiago in the early eleventh century; and William VIII, who led the first Spanish crusade in 1063.[29]

All these Williams provide the fragments out of which *The Crowning* constructs an identity and a persona for Count William. Thus, we see that the epic is the place, the ground, where bits of history gather to form a constellation which addresses the concerns of the twelfth century.

Since *The Crowning* is a composite of many fragments, likewise there is a mosaic of themes that provide an ideological backbone to the work and give it significance.

It would be simple to assume that the ideology of *The Crowning* is Christian vigor, and by extension regal authority. However, there is another far more powerful ethos at play in the poem, one that subsumes religion and kingship, interprets behavior and attitudes, and determines piety and impiety. It is the ideology of the warrior. The particulars of this ideology are the defense and protection of society, defense of the faith, annihilation of enemies, and maintenance of order and peace.[30] The power of the church is subservient to this ideology because without the coercive apparatus (the warrior), the church cannot maintain its role in the medieval world (as the church militant), especially since it faces continual threats from the forces of chaos, such as the Saracens. Consequently, the church legitimizes the use of force (in its capacity to forgive bloodshed)—whether that force is used against Saracens or against Christian rebels who want to subvert society as governed by divine order.

The play of warrior ideology achieves greater power when we consider *The Crowning* as concerned with maintaining social order, which in the medieval mind consisted of a pyramidical descent of power: There was God in heaven, the church in the world, the king in his country, the barons in their fiefs, and the laborers on the land. Just as God with his might held together his heavenly realm, so the warrior with his strength held together the earthly realm. (And here we must keep in mind that the king rightly belongs to the warrior class and as such is the first among equals.) Without the ethos of the warrior, society faced utter turmoil. Hence, the warrior is the centrifugal force of the epic. Without William's strength Louis would lose his crown, Rome would fall to the Saracens, Corsolt would win, the Pope would be humiliated, the church would be desecrated, and God Himself would be routed from the earth (Corsolt's great vaunt).

Certainly, it is with Corsolt that William has his greatest battle, one that defines him as a great warrior. And Corsolt is a Saracen. To the audience of *The Crowning* this word was synonymous with the Muslims, against whom Europe was then sending out Crusades, missions of "rescue" of the Holy Land from infidel hands. And because Muslims were seen as infidels, they were perceived as godless heathens to whom all manner of outlandish beliefs could be ascribed, with no basis in reality. *The Crowning* tells us the Saracens worship various gods (including Mahomet) that are little better than devils. There is little real interest in the Saracens as such; they are merely the enemy, "the bad guys" against and upon whom noble Christian warriors can demonstrate their own righteous and pious prowess. In short, Saracens made good entertainment.[31] Therefore, when Corsolt appears as the champion of the Saracens, he is described as a monster, not only in belief but also in appearance (perhaps the one led to the other according to medieval thinking). He is a giant, disfigured, immensely strong, most certainly a cannibal, and he is the avowed enemy of the Christian God, whom he has "banished" to heaven, while the earth he has claimed as his own. Therefore anyone who worships God on earth is his enemy, for on earth he is god.

Since *The Crowning* is about war and the ethos of the warrior, William is pitted against this hideous enemy. Before he encounters Corsolt in battle, William utters a very lengthy prayer (ll. 695–789). This prayer summarizes the life of Christ and concludes with a request for aid in battle against the deadly and heathen foe. This prayer serves to remind us that in the medieval mind Christ, like William, was a heroic character who struggled for God on the earth, just as William now must fight for God against Corsolt. Thus there is a link between the deeds of Christ and the deeds of William; the battlefield is the site where mythic and historical fragments become constructs of the constellation of the hero's *raison d'être:* war.

In the life of the hero, one battle marks him.[32] And for William it is his single combat with Corsolt. After he slays the giant, he carries a mark that will stay with him, even define him: he will be "William Shortnose" forever. But this is not merely an old "war wound"; it is also a sign of William's piety, for battling heathens is a religious task and a spiritual struggle. His mark is like the five wounds of Christ, which Jesus bore in his battle against the heathens of his day. This move to spiritualize violence (again stressing the need of the church for the warrior) is propounded by a great personality of the time, St. Bernard of Clairvaux, in the treatise entitled *In Praise of the New Knighthood,* which he wrote around 1130.[33]

St. Bernard wrote to support the Templar Knights (his pet project) and also to encourage the fight against Muslims in the Holy Land. St. Bernard undertakes a hermeneutics of transposition, giving knightly virtue and valor a spiritual meaning and interpretation. He tells us that violence should be channeled for the work of God and defense of the faith: Bernard wants warriors to become *militia Christi*.

Similarly, *The Crowning* proposes a secular and a sacred hermeneutics of violence. On the spiritual plane the warrior must fight for God and the faith, vanquishing Saracens or at least converting them (*The Crowning* allows both); on the secular level the warrior must battle those who seek to usurp the power of the legitimate king.

Within the context of the warrior-based society portrayed in *The Crowning*, we find that the primary concerns of the epic are faith, combat and reward. All three are a triadic unity in that they are intertwined; St. Bernard's hermeneutics is certainly at play here. We see that faith sustains William and gives him an ideology wherein he can justify his violence and bloodshed as pious acts. It is for God that he fights, and Louis is God's anointed king; thus it is William's religious duty to protect the king from traitors, just as he must protect the Pope and Christianity from the onslaught of the Saracens. The task of protection involves combat and violence. Therefore the inherent responsibility of the warrior (to fight and protect) is channeled into spiritual duty. Throughout the epic, then, William practices a piety of violence, for it is through acts of aggression and bloodshed that William seeks to perfect himself and achieve his reward: a fief of his own, and salvation. *The Crowning* melds the ethos of the warrior with the demands of militant Christianity.

The Crowning is written in *langue d'oïl*, or Old French spoken in northern France. Translating from languages that are long extinct is a unique task, for it provides the text with an afterlife: We place the dead language within the constellation of a living one. Like history itself, a dead language is also a fragment from the past whose context we can never fully know. For example, we can try to approximate the pronunciation of words, but we can never know the mind that used this language to express being and consciousness; we may adequately express all the content of the text, and yet an element will remain beyond the reach of all translations. The original is certainly a compact unit, wherein there is perfect harmony of language and content. However, when we translate we are forever placing the content into an alien language (context), very much like ancient artifacts in a museum: None of the things displayed were meant for museums; they were objects of daily life. Translation, in short, is the *parousia* (the presence in the present) of language. And *The Crowning* is an echo from the twelfth century. The task of the translator, then, is to give further resonance to this echo—to allow the modern world to hear some trace of it, just as we can still see the light of stars long dead.

A word on the notes to the translation: A boldface number in the right-hand margin indicates an endnote related to that line of the poem. Numbers not in boldface are simple place-markers for reference purposes.

Notes

1. The provenance can be deduced from the language of the poem, which is *langue d'oïl*, a dialect of Old French spoken in northern France, particularly Picardy and Ile-de-France (the region surrounding Paris). For a fuller discussion, see A. Hindley and B. Levy, *The Old French Epic: An Introduction* (Louvain: Peeters, 1983).

2. The nine manuscripts are: Paris, Bib. Nat. Fr. 774, Fol. 18–33 (13th century); Paris Bib. Nat. Fr. 1149, Fol. 23–38 (13th century); Paris, Bib. Nat. Fr. 368, Fol. 161–162 (a mutilated 13th century manuscript containing only 597 lines); Milan, Bib. Trivulzienne, Fol. 22–38 (13th century); Boulogne-sur-Mer Bib. Communale, S. Bertin 192, Fol. 21–38 (13th century); Paris Bib. Nat., nouv. acq. Fr. 5094 (a fragment from the 13th century, with 14 lines recto and 15 lines verso); Paris Bib. Nat. Fr. 1448, Fol. 88–89 (a very different 13th century version of only 316 lines closely linked to another verse epic, *Charroi de Nimes*); Paris, Bib. Nat. Fr. 24369, Fol. 75–90 (14th century); London, British Library, 20 D XI, Fol. 103–112 (14th century).

3. The word *jongleur* stems from the Latin *joculator* ("jester" or "comedian") and the Old High German *jangler* ("moaner" or "yelper"). This gave rise in the twelfth century to the term *jongleur*. In England, the term used for these entertainers was "gleemen" ("merrymen"). *Jongleurs* were wandering performers: they played various instruments, they sang, juggled, did magic tricks, and staged mimes. They belonged to the lowest rung of medieval society; female *jongleurs* routinely practiced prostitution. Further details can be found in Jeremy Yudkin, *Music in Medieval Europe* (Englewood Cliffs, N.J.: Prentice Hall, 1989), Elizabeth Aubrey, *The Music of the Troubadours* (Bloomington: Indiana University Press, 1996), and Edmond Faral, *Les jongleurs en France au moyen age* (Paris: H. Champion, 1964).

4. See Edward A. Heinemann, *L'art métrique de la chanson de geste: essai sur la musicalité du récit* (Geneva: Librairie Droz, 1993) and Claude Riot, *Chants et instruments: trouvères et jongleurs au moyen age* (Paris: R.E.M.P.A.R.T., 1995).

5. For studies on oral literature, see Walter J. Ong, *Orality and Literacy* (London and New York: Methuen, 1982), and the classic study by Albert B. Lord, *The Singer of Tales* (Cambridge, MA and London, UK: Harvard University Press, 1960).

6. For further details, see R.N. Swanson, *The Twelfth-Century Renaissance* (Manchester; New York: Manchester University Press, 1999) and Peter Damian-Grint, *The New Historians of the Twelfth-Century Renaissance: Inventing Vernacular Authority* (Woodbridge, Suffolk; Rochester, N.Y.: Boydell Press, 1999).

7. The earliest *chanson de geste* is the anonymous *Song of Roland*, which was written down around 1000 – 1010. In all some 120 *chansons de geste* have come down to us.

8. For a full reassessment of Louis the Pious see Peter Godman and Roger

Collins, eds., *Charlemagne's Heir: New Perspectives on the Reign of Louis the Pious. 814–840* (Oxford and New York: Clarendon Press, 1990).

9. This reading stems from Augustine's *Confessions*, trans. R. Warner. New York: New American Library, 1963. It can be said that Augustine embarks on a hermeneutic of the spirit, bringing together Platonic and Neoplatonic as well as Judeo-Christian ideas in order to achieve a synthetic understanding of God's role in history. The methodology he employs in his peculiar synthesis is typology, which teaches that things and events are signs that point to the hidden meaning within. Thus, in history nothing is what it appears to be, for it must always already be the other.

10. This should not be construed as sexism, but the inevitable result of the epics that we possess. The hero in these works is invariably male.

11. By tropology I mean not only a moral discourse, but also the use of metaphors (tropes) in writing.

12. Martin Heidegger uses the term *alétheia* to address the revelation (unconcealedness) of Being. See Martin Heidegger, *Poetry, Language, Thought*, trans. A. Hofstader (New York: Harper & Row, 1971), pp. 17–18.

13. See "Epic and Novel" in M.M. Bakhtin, *The Dialogic Imagination*, ed. Michael Holquist, trans. Caryl Emerson and Michael Holquist (Austin: University of Texas Press, 1987), pp. 3–40.

14. See M.M. Bakhtin, "From the Prehistory of Novelistic Discourse," in Holquist (1987), pp. 41–83.

15. See Walter Benjamin, "Theses on the Philosophy of History," in *Illuminations*, Ed. Hannah Arendt (New York: Schocken Books, 1969), p. 263.

16. For a detailed look at the life of Louis the Pious see Egon Boshof, *Ludwig der Fromme* (Darmstadt: Primus, 1996).

17. For Louis the Pious' relationship with the church, see Thomas F.X. Noble's PhD dissertation entitled *Louis the Pious and the Papacy: Law, Politics and the Theory of Empire in the Early Ninth Century* (Michigan State University, 1974).

18. For a contemporary view of Louis the Pious see Thegan's *Gesta Hludowici Imperatoris* and Astronomus' *Vita Hludowici Imperatoris* in *Die Taten Kaiser Ludwigs*, trans. Ernst Tremp, Monumenta Germaniae Historica, 64 (Hanover: Hahnsche Buchhandlung, 1995).

19. For a contemporary assessment of Louis VI's life see Abbot Suger's *The Deeds of Louis the Fat*, trans. Richard Cusimano and John Moorhead (Washington, DC: Catholic University of America Press, 1992). See also John Bell Henneman, *The Medieval French Monarchy* (Hinsdale, Ill: Dryden Press, 1973).

20. Louis VII was crowned only after his older brother Philippe (who had earlier been crowned king by Louis the Fat) had suddenly died in 1131. This revived the desires of other barons to take the French throne. In order to quash the hopes of these barons, Louis the Fat quickly moved to have his younger son crowned as Louis VII.

21. Before he died, Louis the Fat also arranged the marriage of his son to Eleanor of Aquitaine, who brought southwest France to the realm of the new French king. Eleanor was not faithful, and Louis VII found controlling his jealousy difficult. But he was a very religious man, and sought to do pious acts, which would help his marriage. Thus, he left for the Second Crusade in 1147 and took

Eleanor with him. After failing miserably in the Holy Land, he returned to France and had his marriage annulled in 1152. Soon thereafter, Eleanor proposed marriage to Henry, Count of Anjou and Duke of Normandy. Henry immediately accepted, and the two married; Eleanor took southwest France with her. Two years later, Henry (II) and Eleanor became king and queen of England. It was Henry II who had Thomas Becket murdered.

22. Marie-Hélène Jullien and Françoise Perelman, eds., *Clavis scriptorum latinorum medii aevi: auctores galliae, 735–987* (Turnholti: Brepols, 1994).

23. *Chronicon Moissiacense*, ed. Georg Heinrich Pertz, Monumenta Germaniae Historica, SS, tome 1 (Hanover: Impensis Bibliopolii Hahniani, 1826).

24. Demaso Alonso, *La Primitiva Epica Francesa a la Luz de una Nota Emilianense* (Madrid: Instituto Miguel de Cervantes, 1954).

25. For a translation of the Hague Fragment see Martín de Riquer, *Les chansons de geste françaises* (Paris: Nizet, 1957).

26. *The Ecclesiastical History of Orderic Vitalis*, ed. and trans. Marjorie Chibnall, Vol. 1 (Oxford: Chibnall Press, 1980).

27. See the *Vita domni Willelmi Abbatis* by Rodolfus Glaber (ca. 985–1047) in *The Five Books of the Histories and The Life of Saint William*, eds. and trans. John France and Paul Reynolds (Oxford: Clarendon Press, 1989).

28. For an account of the Dukes of Aquitaine see Charles Higounet, *Histoire de l'Aquitaine* (Toulouse: Privat, 1971). Also see Alfred Jeanroy, *Les chansons de Guillaume IX duc d'Aquitaine, 1071–1127* (Paris: Champion, 1913).

29. Michel Dillange, *Les comtes de Poitou: ducs d'Aquitaine 778–1204* (Mougons: Geste editions, 1995).

30. The discussion that follows derives from the monumental study of Indo-European society by Georges Dumézil, especially his *The Destiny of the Warrior*, trans. Alf Hiltebeitel (Chicago and London: The University of Chicago Press, 1970), and *The Destiny of a King*, trans. Alf Hiltebeitel (Chicago and London: The University of Chicago Press, 1973). Although I have avoided applying a strict Dumézilian reading of *The Crowning*, there are marked Indo-European elements that may be analyzed, such as the implied cowardice of William, the sin of William (mutilation of Richard of Rouen and the killing of his son), and the sign of the warrior (William's cut nose).

31. The portrayal of the Saracens (and Muslim culture and belief) in the *chansons de geste* is discussed in Norman Daniel's *Heroes and Saracens* (Edinburgh: Edinburgh University Press, 1984).

32. Dumézil (1970), pp. 161–164.

33. Saint Bernard, *On Grace and Free Choice. In Praise of the New Knighthood*, trans. Conrad Greenia, Introduction by R.J. Zwi Weblowsky (Kalamazoo: Cistercian Publications, 1977).

The Crowning of Louis

1

Listen, lords, and may God grant you His aid!
Will it please you to hear a high, bold tale,
A good song of courtesy and prowess?
Why should a common minstrel boast and vaunt?
Each word he speaks is uttered by command. 5
I shall not fail to sing you of Louis,
And of William Shortnose, the most gallant,
Who suffered sore, fighting the Saracens.
Of no better man can I sing for you.

2

Lord barons, do you seek an example 10
Of a song well-constructed and pleasing?
When God came to choose the ninety-nine realms, 12
The best of all things He placed in sweet France.
The greatest of kings was named Charlemagne,
Who magnified sweet France with all his heart: 15
God did not make a land not bound to him.
Bavaria and Germany are his,
As are Normandy, Anjou, Brittany,
Lombardy, Navarre, also Tuscany. 19

3

The king who wears the golden crown of France 20
Must be prudent and valiant in his heart;

For if any man sought to do him harm,
No wood or plain could hide that wretched man:
The king would find him out and then slay him.
If he failed in this, France would lose honor; 25
History would call him "The Wrongly Crowned."

4

When the church was consecrated at Aix, 27
And the chapel had been dedicated,
The court assembled, splendid beyond words:
Fourteen counts alone guarded the palace. 30
And the poor then gathered to seek justice;
None departed without proper redress.
Then, justice was given — now no longer:
For the wicked have now all turned to greed,
And false judgments have silenced the good plea. 35
But God is just who rules and gives us life:
He punishes all the wicked in Hell —
That horrid hole from which no one returns.

5

Now that day, there were eighteen good bishops,
And there were eighteen good archbishops, too. 40
The Apostle of Rome did sing the Mass. 41

6

That day, the offertory was splendid, 42
For none better was ever heard in France.
Those who partook of it obtained great joy.

7

Now, that day, there were twenty-six abbots; 45
Also on that day there were four crowned kings.
On that day Louis was elevated,
And the crown was placed upon the altar;

The King his father had ordained the day.
Then one archbishop mounted the lectern 50
And gave the sermon to all the Christians.
"Barons," he said, "Lend me your attention.
Charlemagne has exhausted all his days,
And he can no longer live as before.
No more shall he wear the bright crown henceforth. 55
He has a son to whom he shall give it."
When they heard this, the barons were joyful;
Then all of them stretched out their hands to God:
"Father of glory, You are merciful,
For You will not send us a foreign king!" 60
Our Emperor called out to his son:
"My good son," he said, "Listen to my words.
Behold the crown that lies on the altar.
I shall give it to you on one demand:
Do not be wicked, lustful, or sinful; 65
Be not treacherous to any person,
Nor abandon orphans in your fiefdom.
If you agree, I praise our lord God,
And take up the crown, for you will be crowned.
If not, my son, leave it where it now lies, 70
For I forbid you to even touch it. 71

8

"My son, Louis. Behold, here is the crown.
Take it, and become Emperor of Rome.
Yours are a hundred thousand men at arms
To cross the deep waters of the Gironde, 75
And crush and destroy the pagan people,
And then take all their lands as our own.
If you do this, I will give you the crown;
If not, then you shall never have the crown.

9

"If, good son, you are paid for false judgment, 80
And favor and honor the vain and proud;

If you are lustful and exalt sinners,
And neglect all orphans in your fiefdom,
And cannot spare four deniers for widows— 84
Then, by Jesus, I forbid you this crown, 85
My son Louis—do not reach out for it."
The lad heard these words and came not forward.
A great many gallant knights wept for him,
And the Emperor was irate, enraged.
"Alas!" he said, "how have I been deceived! 90
A paltry rogue must have slept with my wife
And engendered this most cowardly heir.
Never in his life will he be like me.
To make him king will be the greatest sin.
Thus, let us now cut off all of his hair 95
And send him off to a monastery,
Where he will pull ropes and be a warden. 97
He'll deal with prebends so as not to beg." 98
Arnéïs d'Orléans sat by the King,
Who was a proud and vainglorious man; 100
He spoke these great words of cunning to him:
"True Emperor, calm yourself, and hear me.
Our prince is young and not yet fifteen.
He'd soon be dead, if you made him a knight. 104
If you so wish, grant me charge of the realm 105
For three years, in which time I will test him.
If he proves gallant and a fitting heir,
Gladly shall I return the realm to him,
And add more to his lands and his fiefdoms."
The King said to him, "I'm in agreement." 110
"Hearty thanks, Sire," said the flatterers,
Who were kin of Arnéïs d'Orléans.
King they sought to make him — then William came,
Returning from a hunt in the forest.
His nephew Bertrand ran, held the stirrups. 115
He asked him, "Whence have you come, good nephew?"
"In God's name, Sire, from within the church,
Where I did see great injustice and sin.
Arnéïs has betrayed his rightful lord.
Soon he'll be king, as the Franks have deemed it." 120
"Bad luck for him," said William the gallant.
With his sword girded, he entered the church;

He pressed through the crowd and went to the front,
And found Arnéïs all pompously dressed.
He sought to cut off his head right away. 125
But he thought of the wondrous Lord on high:
For killing a man is the greatest sin.
He did not take out his sword from its sheath,
But came forward and rolled up both his sleeves.
Then with his left hand he grabbed the rogue's hair, 130
Raised his right hand and struck him at the neck,
And so shattered the bone that lies within.
Thus by this blow he fell dead at his feet.
Having killed him, he threw insults at him:
"Ah, brigand!" he said, "thus has God paid you! 135
Why did you choose to betray your true lord?
You should have sought to love and cherish him;
Enlarged his lands; gathered fiefdoms for him.
And now look where your falseness has brought you:
For I had only meant to chastise you — 140
But now you lie dead, not worth a denier."
He saw the crown lying on the altar;
Without hesitation, he took it up,
Came to the lad and placed it on his head.
"Take this, lord, in the name of Heaven's King, 145
And may He grant you the strength to be just!"
This made the father rejoice for his son:
"Lord William, you are most gratefully thanked —
Your kinsfolk shall be highest, after mine."

10

"Ah, Louis," said Charles, "my good, noble son, 150
Now you shall come to govern my kingdom;
And may you hold it when it is your turn:
Never withhold the orphan from his rights,
Nor an Angevin mite from a widow. **154**
Always remember to serve Holy Church, 155
So that the Devil may not bring you shame.
Forget not to hold and cherish your knights,
For through them you shall be honored and served.
Thus shall you be loved, cherished in the land."

11

When the crowning day of Louis was done,   160
The court dispersed and the audience left.
Each Frank then returned to his house and hearth.   162
Afterwards, Charles lived on for five more years.
Charles the King, once, went up to his palace
Where he saw his son and spoke thus to him: 165

12

"Son Louis, I cannot hide this from you:
You are going to possess my kingdom
After my death, if God thus blesses me.
Those who fought me, I know, will defy you;
Those who hate me, I know, will not love you.   170
If I catch them, by God, son of Mary,
I shall not seek to get ransom for them —
But slay them and tear them all to pieces.

13

"Son Louis, I cannot hide this from you:
When God made kings to rule over people   175
He left no room for them to judge falsely,
Nor to be lustful, nor even sinful,
Nor to banish orphans from their kingdoms,
Nor to tax widows, even four deniers.
Rather a king should strike down injustice,   180
Smashing and stamping it into the earth.
Now, always be humble with the poor.
Let not their pleas move you to great anger —
But you must lend them help with good council,
For the love of God, give them all their rights.   185
Against the vain you must be ferocious,
Like a leopard that devours people.   187
And if it is that you need to make war,
Beckon from France knights that are most noble,
Of which you have about thirty thousand.   190
And where you want to lay siege, if you wish,
You must ravage, devastate all the land.

If you want to take it into your hand,
you must show neither pity nor mercy:
Cut off the limbs of the inhabitants, 195
Burn them with fire, drown them in water. **196**
Thus should the Franks see you trampling others.
Now the Normans, they will say in reproach: **198**
'We have no need for such a king as this,
May misfortune strike the top of the head 200
Of the man who goes to join his campaigns,
Or goes to his court to be a courtier.
We would only be serving for his good.'
One more advice I shall give you, my son,
Which you will find to be valuable: 205
Take not an evil man as counselor,
Neither a provost nor a warden's son— **207**
He will always betray you for money.
But take William the good and bold warrior,
Son of Aimeri of Narbonne, the proud, 210
Brother of the bold Bernard of Brabant—
He will support you and give you great aid.
Have complete confidence in his service."
The lad said: "You speak the truth, by my head."
He went to the Count and fell at his feet. 215
But good William stood him back on his feet,
And said to him: "Young lord, what do you want?"
"In God's name, sir, I want help and pity.
My father said that you are the best knight—
No other baron beneath the sky's dome. 220
To you I confer my lands and fiefdoms,
Which you will guard well for me, noble knight,
Until I can carry my own armor."
The Count replied: "I'll do this, by my faith."
He swore to him by the saints of the church: 225
He would not keep back even four deniers,
If they were not freely given to him.
He then went up to Charles without delay.
He went down on his knees before the King.
"True Emperor, I ask of you this wish. 230
I want to go away at once and ride
Straight out to Rome and pray to Saint Peter.
As you know, it has been now fifteen years

That I made a vow to go, but could not.
I can put off this voyage no longer." 235
Ruefully and sadly the King agreed.
He placed under his command sixty knights,
Thirty mules laden with gold and silver.
When he left they did run to embrace him.
In this way did the brave warrior ride off. 240
But great hardships would hinder his return.
Charles would be dead by the time he came back;
Louis living on his inheritance.
Before William could take any action—
For freely he could not return to France— 245
Louis would be unjustly locked away,
Expecting to have all his limbs hacked off—
For him William might be delayed too long.

14

Thus, William Strongarm went up to the church,
And did ask leave of the Emperor Charles 250
Who placed sixty men of arms under him,
And thirty mules packed with silver and gold.
Off went the Count, without any delay,
And escorted Louis back, at long last.
Weeping, he called out to William Strongarm: 255
"Ah, Count, in the name of God the Spirit; **256**
Behold my father has renounced the world;
Old and feeble, he cannot carry arms—
And I am still young, not yet come of age.
If I do not have succor, all is lost." 260
The Count replied: "Do not be uneasy,
For by all the relics of Saint Peter,
When I do undertake this pilgrimage,
And you summon me by charter and seal, **264**
Or by a messenger worthy of trust, 265
I know of no man who will hinder me
From coming to your aid with my barons."
Then the Count left without further delay.
I cannot recount all his daily deeds.
He crossed Montjeu—that was a hard passage. 270
Strongarm did not rest until he reached Rome.

15

Now, with good William, the most gallant, went
Both Guiélin and Bertrand the renowned.
Underneath their cloaks they wore enchased glaives. 274
As well, they had trussed up all their baggage, 275
And their well-linked hauberks and gilded helms. 276
The pages were greatly fraught with fatigue
By bearing the great shields, the long lances. 278
I cannot recount all their daily deeds.
They crossed over Montjeu with great hardship, 280
And made their way slowly through Romany.
Now they did not stop until they reached Rome.
The pages procured suitable lodgings.
Now, the name of their good host was Ciquaire,
To whom William gave over his fortune. 285
That night indeed the Count was well treated.
After eating, they all took their repose—
Deeply slept the Count; great was his fatigue.
He had a dream that filled him with great dread: 289
From Russia did emerge blazing fire, 290
The flames of which encircled all of Rome.
Then a wolfhound came running at full speed; 292
Some he left, while others he tore apart.
William stood beneath a large spreading tree: 294
This beast filled him with terror and great dread, 295
For with its paw it gave him such a blow
That he was knocked down flat upon the earth.
The Count awoke, and put his trust in God.
No previous dream made this point clear:
All the Saracens were on a campaign— 300
Both King Galafrez and King Tenebrez;
The King Cremuz and the Emir Corsolt.
These lords had seized the fort at Capua,
And good King Guaifier was now held captive,
With his daughter and wife of great beauty. 305
Thirty thousand unfortunate captives
Were led off—all soon to be beheaded.
William the renowned was most loved by God,
For he went and delivered the captives
When he battled Corsolt by the Red Sea— 310

That great, strong man of whom we have heard much.
He did strike at William and cut his nose,
As you shall soon learn before the night falls—
If you give me enough that I may sing. 314
So it was that the day began to dawn. 315
Count William rose early in the morning;
He went to church to attend the service. 317
All his arms he placed upon the altar; 318
With Arabian gold he would free them. 319
The Pope, who was noble and most gallant, 320
Was now richly arrayed to sing the Mass.
When the service was all said and finished,
Two messengers came who had ridden hard.
Soon enough they recounted all the news.
Now, that day frightened many a free man. 325

16

William Strongarm had gone up to the church;
The Pope with great wisdom had sung the Mass.
When he finished, two messengers arrived,
Who brought with them unfortunate reports:
The Saracens they said had brought great harm, 330
Capturing Capua, the great city,
And taking thirty thousand prisoners,
Who would all die by fire if not saved.
The Pope was shaken and greatly distressed,
So he wanted to see William Strongarm. 335
They pointed him out on the floor below,
Where he was praying to God the Father
That He grant him and his true lord Louis,
The son of Charles, strength, honor and courage.
The Pope, without showing hesitation, 340
Took his staff and touched him on the shoulder; 341
Then the Count rose up and showed him his face.

17

Now Count William stood back up on his feet,
And the Pope spoke to him in this manner:

"Ah, most gentle man, in the name of God, 345
Tell me if you are able to help me.
Pagans and other foes have besieged us,
And King Galafrez is their mighty king.
We must help and aid all who are in need:
For good King Guaifier was taken by force, 350
Along with his daughter and noble wife,
And thirty thousand ill-fated captives—
If not rescued, they will all lose their heads.
"God help them," said the Count with the brave face. 354
He crossed himself thinking of all the kings. 355
Now Bertrand his nephew said in reproach:
"Uncle William, have you lost all your wits?
Never have I seen you dread any man."
William said, "Thank you, good nephew, by God,
Against all their might ours is nothing. 360
We must at once search out a messenger,
And we must send a letter to Louis
To come to our aid and bring relief. 363
Charles can stay in France to mete out justice:
Old and frail is he, unable to ride." 365
Bertrand replied, "May the God of justice
Confound and kill, or drive utterly mad
That man who would carry such a message!
And may that man's shield shatter and splinter,
And his hauberk loosen and unravel, 370
And he himself be struck down by a lance —
This should be the fate of such an envoy!
Pagans beset us by hundreds, thousands.
Quickly to arms now! We must not tarry!
We must guard ourselves without delay!" 375
The Romans were in very great anguish;
They had few men — not hundreds of thousands.

18

Now the brave-faced Count was inside the church.
The Pope, most wise and gallant, said to him:
"Noble man, by God who is pure spirit, 380
Deliver us from these savage people."

"Ah, may God help us," said the Count Strongarm.
"For I came here only on pilgrimage;
And I brought very few warriors with me —
I do not have more than sixty armed knights. 385
I cannot fight against all those great kings."
"Alas, God help us," said the Pope, most wise.
"Here is Saint Peter, the warden of souls:
If today you do this service for him,
You shall have bread to eat all your life long, 390
And shall take to wife the woman you want.
No sin shall bind you, no matter how grave,
Only if you keep yourself from treason —
And do not swerve from this for all your life.
You shall secure your place in paradise — 395
That place which our Lord keeps for His friends.
And there, Saint Gabriel shall be your guide."
"Now may God help us," said the Count Strongarm.
"No priest can have a more generous heart!
Indeed, I do not know of any man, 400
Not even a harsh, treacherous pagan,
Who can now keep me back from this great fight.
Good nephew, Bertrand, come take up your arms!
You too, Guiélin; and all you barons!"
William Strongarm called out for his great arms; 405
These they brought him; placed them in front of him.
He donned his hauberk, laced his green helmet,
And girded his sword with clasps of pure silk. **408**
They brought beside him his white-stockinged horse,
And he leaped on without using stirrups. 410
Around his neck he hung a bright red targe, **411**
And took up a stout, sharp lance in his hand;
With five golden studs he fixed his standard. **413**
"Lord Pope," said good William, the most noble,
"How many men have you in your demesne?" 415
The Pope replied, "I shall tell you plainly:
We are three thousand; none without helmet,
And a sturdy lance and a sharp-edged sword."
The Count responded, "This is a good start.
Let them arm themselves. And all those on foot 420
Will go to guard the gates and the ramparts."
The Pope said to him: "This is the right thing."

Now all over Rome men took up their arms;
Then they went and took up their positions.
The Pope blessed them with the sign of the cross. 425
"Lord barons," said the Pope most sagacious,
"He who will die in battle on this day
Shall surely have his place in paradise —
That place which our Lord keeps for His friends.
And there, Saint Gabriel shall be his guide." 430
Then they arose; each one took up his arms
To fight the wretched and savage people.
Then they all assembled, clashing their arms, **433**
There at the grand gates, which were very high.
"Lord barons," said the Pope most sagacious, 435
"Protect these men at arms all gathered here,
I shall now speak with Emir Galafrez. **437**
If he were promised a great many goods,
He may turn back with his ships and barges,
And his countless troops that are marshaled here: 440
To him I shall give Saint Peter's treasure, **441**
Withholding neither chalice nor mantle,
Gold nor silver, nor anything of worth —
Rather than have great men of valor die."
They replied: "This is the right thing to do." 445
Then he left, taking an abbot with him,
And he went up and stood before their tents,
Where he found the mighty King Galafrez.
He did not greet him, deeming it unfit.
The mighty King looked at him angrily. 450
Straightaway, the Pope said these words to him:
"Lord," he said, "I come as a messenger
Of God and Saint Peter, the ward of souls.
On his behalf I give you this message:
Depart with all your ships and your barges, 455
And your countless troops that are marshaled here.
To you I shall give Saint Peter's treasure,
Withholding neither chalice nor mantle,
Gold nor silver, nor anything of worth —
Rather than have great men of valor die. 460
Take good heed, gentle and most noble king."
The King replied: "You are not very wise,
For I came here to claim my true birthright — **463**

Given me by all my great forefathers,
And by Romulus and Julius Caesar, 465
Who built these walls, these gates, and these ramparts.
If by force I can knock down these pillars,
All those who reach out to God will suffer;
Priests who serve Him will be beaten and shamed."
At these words, the Pope was filled with great rage; 470
Would not stay for all the gold of Carthage, **471**
And sought escort from Emir Galafrez.
He got three Saracens for safe conduct.
The King Galafrez again said to him:
"Speak with me, O great lord of the large hat. 475
Say not to me that I have been unjust
To this city — my true inheritance.
Choose a man fully arrayed in his arms,
And I shall choose one from my great household:
As combatants shall they meet on the field. 480
If your God is mighty enough to act,
So that my champion is conquered by yours,
Then shall Rome be your rightful heritage.
Now you shall not soon find in all your life
Such gain for the paltry price of a cheese. 485
And if at some point I fail my promise,
Take and hold my two sons as hostages,
For whom any ransom shall be worthless—
Rather you may hang them both from a tree." **489**
Glad was the Pope when he heard this sage thought, 490
As if given all the gold of Carthage.
Then did he remember the Count Strongarm, 492
All armed in the church before the altar.
None was better than him that carried arms. **494**

19

The Pope was a very insightful man: 495
He could see that God wanted to help him,
Letting him defend his cause through a man.
Thus he upheld his cause before the foe:
"Sire," said he, "I hide not this from you,
We must protect our rights through two men. 500

Willingly shall I behold your champion,
Who would now challenge Rome against God's will."
The King replied: "That is easily done."
Then they brought King Corsolt, right at his feet: **504**
Squint-eyed, ugly, gruesome as the Devil; 505
His eyes red as coals in a brazier;
His face grossly huge; his head all bristled;
His two eyes were set half-a-foot apart;
Two yards wide from the waist to the shoulders.
A more unsightly man never broke bread. 510
He began to roll his eyes at the Pope,
And bellowed: "Little man, what do you want?
Do you now want your sanctity tonsured?" **513**
"Sir," he replied, "I serve God in the church,
God above and Saint Peter, our lord. 515
On his behalf, I now do plead with you
That in good faith you turn back with your host.
I shall give you the church's great treasure:
Not one chalice, incensor shall we keep,
Nor a denier's worth of gold and silver. 520
All this shall I bring out for you to take." **521**
The King replied: "You don't seem well-informed,
You who dare to plead for God before me.
It is men of the world who anger me:
A bolt out of Heaven killed my father— 525
All burned was he; nothing could help save him.
After God killed him, He did something wise—
He went up to the sky; did not return.
I cannot follow Him and hunt Him down;
But I can take revenge on His people. 530
Of those brought before the font and baptized
I have destroyed more than thirty thousand:
Burning by fire, drowning in water.
Since I could not fight with God up above,
I will not spare His people here below. 535
God and I no longer have a quarrel:
The earth belongs to me, Heaven to Him. **537**
If by force I take this territory,
I shall destroy all that belongs to God,
And flay with a knife all priests who serve Him. 540
As for you, who are the head of the church,

I shall roast you over coals in a hearth
Till your liver falls on the heap of coals." 543
When the Pope heard him speak in this manner,
He did not marvel but became frightened. 545
Then he and the Abbot both took counsel:
"By Saint Denis, this Turk is fully mad!
Great marvel earth is still under his feet
And God has not sent him into Hell's flames. 549
Ah, good William! O most brave-faced Marquis, 550
May He, who was stretched on the cross, guard you!
You may not have much more against this Turk!"
He asked for safe-conduct from Galafrez
The proud, who gave him his two sons and wife.
Up to Rome they led him, walking on foot. 555
Now Count William was the first to meet him,
And he seized the metal of his stirrups.
"Sire," said he, "how went your embassy?
And tell me, have you seen the enemy
Who would fight with Rome, much against God's will? 560
Noble lord, have you negotiated?"
"Yes, good sir, I cannot hide this from you:
He's not human, but the Devil himself.
If Roland and Olivier were alive,
Yves and Yvoire, Haton and Béranger, 565
And the Archbishop and young Manessier,
Estolt de Langres, courteous Gautier,
With Gérin and Angelier among them,
The Twelve Peers that fled the massacre;
If Aimeri the warrior also came, 570
Your noble father, man of great valor,
And all your brothers who are doughty knights—
All these men could not match him in battle."
"Oh God," said William. "What will happen now?
For I see that the clergy is all lost. 575
Indeed, you have said that God is mighty,
Who ever sustains and helps his people,
Whom none can dishonor or put to shame,
Nor burn in fire or drown in water.
By the Apostle we pray to in Rome, 580
Though this pagan were eighty feet bigger,
Still I would fight him with iron and steel!

If God wants to dishonor our faith,
It is best to perish in this struggle.
If He wishes to sustain and aid me, 585
Then no man under Heaven can harm me,
Burn me in fire, drown me in water!"
When the Pope heard him speak in this manner,
"Ah!" said he, "you noble, valiant knight!
May He, who was stretched on the cross, guard you! 590
No knight has ever uttered such bold words.
Where you go, Jesus shall come to your aid,
Since you think of Him and believe in Him."
Saint Peter's arm was brought out from the church; 594
They had covered it with gold and silver. 595
Then they made the Count kiss the forefinger;
They made the sign of the Cross on his helm,
Over his heart, before and behind him.
He had need of such a relic that day.
Thenceforth, no man could ever bring him harm, 600
Except some low, base man, worth two deniers,
Who, far hence, may laugh at the gallant knight. 602
Then William mounted his great battle steed.
Around his neck he hung his strapped long shield;
In his fist he clutched his lance, stout and sharp. 605
He rushed to the combat field, on a knoll.
He drew the glances of all pagan eyes.
They said among them: "Look, a noble knight,
Doughty, high-born, courteous and well-armed.
If he fights a man equal to himself, 610
We shall see a hard struggle from the start.
But against Corsolt, his strength is useless:
He'd not give a mite for fourteen like him."

20

Then King Galafrez emerged from his tent,
Royally dressed, splendidly accoutered. 615
He watched the field and he that was on it.
He said to his men: "The Frank has arrived.
I see him on the field; his shield hangs well.
He it is who will fight mighty Corsolt;

But against him he is small, pitiful.   620
Mohammad and Cahut will be weakened,   621
If he's not quickly vanquished by Corsolt."
The King had him summoned, and he came forth.
The King greeted him with both arms outstretched.
"Good nephew," said he, "most welcome are you!   625
Behold the Frank on the high battlefield.
If he is attacked, he cannot retreat."
Corsolt replied: "He is dead and destroyed.
Now that I see him, I will not delay.
Quick my arms! Why should I tarry longer?"   630
Seven kings, fourteen dukes ran to fetch them,
And laid them out beneath a splendid tree:
Arms, whose kind has never been seen, I think.
If some other man put them on his back,
He'd not move, for all the gold of the world.   635

21

Fourteen kings then armed the adversary.
Across his back they strung a steel cuirass,   637
Over it a white double-mail hauberk.
Then he girded his sword of sharpest steel.
It was eight feet long and half-a-foot wide.   640
He took his bow and lashed on his quiver,
Along with his crossbow and darts of steel;
Well-sharpened were those darts, ready to shoot.
They led Alion, his war-horse, to him.
His horse was astonishingly vicious.   645
So feral was he that I have well heard
He stood eight feet high; none could approach him —
Only grooms and those familiar to him.
He had four darts affixed to his saddle;
From the saddle-horn hung an iron mace.   650
King Corsolt mounted, using the stirrups;
From his neck hung his shield sheathed in pure gold.
His strapped long shield was a full eight feet long;
But he never deigned to carry a lance,
So well arrayed was he with double arms.   655
God! What a horse he had broken and tamed!

Despite the weight the steed ran rapidly;
No fast hare or swift greyhound could beat him.
Facing his uncle, he began to speak
In a mighty voice: "Be still and hear me!" 660
Let all the seneschals now come forward! **661**
Set up the tables and prepare the feast.
We shall not tarry because of this Frank.
Soon enough, I'll kill and dismember him:
For not one half-acre shall his feet walk. 665
I will not even draw out my longsword —
But I will give him a blow with my mace. **667**
I will quickly knock him down from his horse —
Never have I eaten a nobleman!" **669**
The pagans cried: "May Mohammad aid you!" 670
The gathered host began to spur him on.
Then the pagans called out to Mohammad.
At once Count William charged straight at his foe:
Repulsive, ugly and laden with arms.
None will now marvel that he was afraid. 675
He called upon God the all-just Father:
"Saint Mary, now here comes a mighty horse!
He does support a man of great valor.
I must keep from harming him with my arms: **679**
May God, who is the Judge of all, guard him, 680
And keep my sword from doing him some harm!"
These were not the words of cowardly need.

22

Now, William stood on the high battleground,
Armed and girded with most noble weapons.
He saw the pagan coming, all-eager. 685
If he was afraid, he cannot be blamed.
He dismounted from his mighty war-horse.
Towards the orient he turned his face,
And said a prayer most great in power. **689**
No man 'neath the sky to a mother born 690
Who, if he speaks with a sincere heart,
After awaking in the early dawn,
Does not dread the assaults of the Devil. **693**

He called on God with great humility:
"Glorious God, who led me to be born, 695
You fashioned earth according to Your will,
And You closed it all around with water.
You fashioned Adam and then Eve his mate,
And You let them both live in paradise.
The fruits of the trees You gave unto them — 700
Save an apple tree forbidden to them. **701**
But they ate of it by some great folly.
Great shame it brought them, when they could not hide.
Thus they had to abandon paradise
And come to earth, to dig and to labor, 705
And suffer and endure a mortal life.
By great cruelty did Cain kill Abel –
That even the earth had to cry aloud.
That day mankind received a cruel gift:
They could never return whence they had come. 710
O God, those who were born of these people
Did not now seek to serve or honor You:
You brought them all to perish in the Flood.
No one could escape except for Noah,
And all his three sons, each one with his mate. 715
To restore the earth, from each of the beasts
He placed a male and female in the Ark.
O God, from those who were born in that age
Came the Virgin, who possessed great goodness,
And through whom You had Your incarnation. 720
In her, You shaped Your form of flesh and bone,
And of holy blood proclaimed by martyrs.
In Bethlehem, the marvelous city,
There it did please You, true God, to be born,
On Christmas Eve, if truth is to be told. 725
You chose to raise up Saint Anastasia; **726**
She had no hands to honor Your body;
These You gave her, as was her desire.
And then did three kings come to visit You; **729**
They honored You with gold, myrrh and incense. 730
You made them depart by another way,
Because of Herod, who was so cruel,
Who did seek to kill and dismember them.
Then were all the Innocents beheaded —

Thirty thousand, so deem the learned clerks. 735
For thirty-two years, like all mortal men,
You wandered the earth, teaching the people.
Then You went into the desert to fast,
For full forty days that did come to pass;
And You let the Devil carry You up. 740
Then on Palm Sunday, amidst palm branches,
You chose, very God, to enter into
Jerusalem, the marvelous city,
By the Golden Gates which were opened up. 744
You forsook riches—such humility: 745
Your heart ever turned towards the poor;
You did stay at Simon the Leper's house,
Where the twelve Apostles all did gather.
The Magdalene, softly and stealthily,
Slipped beneath the table without a word; 750
With bright tears she washed Your gentle feet,
Proceeded to dry them with her hair.
Thus all her many sins were forgiven.
Then Judas did You an act most cruel:
He went and sold You, in his great folly— 755
For just thirty Methuselah deniers. 756
A kiss gave you over to the false Jews; 757
And tied to a beam, You were sorely scourged.
Then the next day, just as the dawn arose,
They did lead You out unto a high place, 760
To Mount Calvary, so I've heard it named.
They made You carry Your cross on Your back;
Thus You went; clothed in a wretched mantle.
You took not one step, in all truthfulness,
Without being struck or whipped or beaten. 765
Your body suffered on the Holy Cross,
And Your limbs were tortured to exhaustion.
Longinus came up, when it was his time; 768
He had not seen You but had heard You speak.
And then with his lance he pierced Your side: 770
Bright blood and water flowed onto his hands;
He rubbed that on his eyes and saw the light.
With great humility he razed his sins—
Thus were his many sins forgiven him.
Nicodemus together with Joseph 775

Did come to you, like two thieves in the night,
And released Your broken limbs from the Cross.
Then they took You and laid You in the tomb.
But on the third day You rose up again.
At once You took the path that led to Hell, 780
Where You did descend to free all Your friends.
Now that was a very lengthy journey. 782
With surety, good King of Majesty,
Defend my body, preserve it from wounds.
On this day, I must battle a demon, 785
Who is giant of limb and powerful.
Saint Mary, if it pleases you, lend aid,
That cowardice may not overtake me
And be a cause of reproach to my heirs."
Then he crossed himself and stood on his feet. 790
The Saracen came at him at a rush.
Then, on seeing William he said these words:
"Tell me, Frank, and do not hide this from me,
With whom now were you speaking, for so long?"
"Now then," said William, "listen to the truth. 795
To glorious God, the King of Majesty,
That He may guide me, in His great goodness,
So that I may now cut off all your limbs,
And throw you down on the field of battle."
The pagan said: "You are full of folly. 800
Do you think that your God has the power
To defend you against me in battle?"
"O wretch," said William, "God shall ruin you!
Because He will sustain and protect me.
Your great pride will be utterly destroyed." 805
"Indeed," said the Turk, "your thoughts are forceful.
But if you come and adore Mohammad
And abandon and defy your own God,
I shall give you honor and great riches,
Such as never all your forefathers had." **810**
"O wretch," said William, "God shall ruin you!
I will not stand in defiance of God."
"Indeed," said the Turk, "you are most lordly,
For I cannot turn your course from battle.
What is your name? Do not keep it from me." 815
"Now then," said William, "listen to the truth;

I do not hide the truth from any man.
By God, I am known as Marquis William,
The son of Aimeri, old graybeard,
And bright-faced Hermeniart, my good mother; 820
Brother of Bernard of Brabant city,
And of Ernaut of Gironde on the sea;
Brother of Garin, who merits all praise,
And Bovon of Comarchis, the gallant,
And Guibert of Andernas, the last born. 825
Gentle Aimers is also my brother,
Who never enters a house or pitched tent,
And is always exposed to wind and storms, **828**
Ever striking down Saracens and slaves:
No love does he bear for all your people." 830
The pagan heard him; held not back his rage.
He rolled his eyes and raised up his eyebrows:
"Wretched Frank, be doughty and hardy now,
Since your family has killed my kinsmen." **834**

23

The Saracen addressed him savagely: 835
"William, you are filled with great fantasies
When you trust in Him who can do nothing.
God is high above, on the Firmament.
Now, he owns not one acre here on earth —
For here is found Mohammad and his rule. 840
All your Masses and all your sacraments,
Your marriages and all your betrothals,
I value no more than a breath of wind:
Christianity is a great folly!" **844**
"O wretch," said William, "God destroy your flesh! 845
Your religion is completely worthless.
As all people know, Mohammad, no doubt,
Was a prophet of Jesus almighty;
He roamed the earth, preaching among mankind.
First of all, it was to Mecca he went, 850
Where he stumbled and fell, for he was drunk —
He died villainously, eaten by pigs.
He, in whom you believe, had no goodness." **853**

Said the pagan: "Such evil lies you tell.
But if you will follow my commandment, 855
And completely believe in Mohammad
I shall grant you high honor and fiefdoms,
Such as never your noble parents had —
Since you do not come from a high lineage.
Oft have I heard men speak of your prowess. 860
Great shame, if you died here most ignobly.
Tell me, you will do as I say at once,
If not, then you shall die most painfully."
"O wretch," said William, "God bring you to naught!
I like you even less now than before — 865
To threaten is not a sign of boldness." **866**
Swiftly, deftly William mounted his horse,
Touching neither the stirrups nor bridle.
He took his shield and hung it on his neck,
And brandished his sword in furious anger; 870
On his lance he hung his waving standard.
The Saracen looked at him ruthlessly,
And said under his breath, so none heard him:
"By Mohammad, the man that I behold
Is filled with great courage and much boldness." 875
If William had heard all of his thoughts then,
He could have worked out an accord with him,
And brought about a beneficent peace.

24

"Now, then, Frank," said Corsolt the most savage,
"By your God for whom you must do battle, 880
Do you claim Rome as your own heritage?"
"Hear then my response," said the Count Strongarm:
"I shall give battle, on horse and with arms,
In God's name, the Father who is spirit.
To Charles our Emperor belongs Rome, 885
Romany, Tuscany, Calabria,
And all Saint Peter's wealth and offerings,
Which the Pope guards with his authority." **888**
The King replied: "You are not well-informed.
Since you will take this heritage by force, 890

It is right proper that you attack me.
But I shall give you a good advantage.
Now draw out your sword and gird up your arms.
Strike me on my shield, then. I shall not move,
For I wish to see some of your valor— 895
How small men carry themselves in battle."
William said: "Only a fool would hold back!"
He spurred his horse, and covered a mile fast
By the hill, which was broad and expansive.
All about him he had girded his arms. 900
The Saracen did not budge from his place.
The Pope said: "Now shall the battle begin.
Kneel thus on the ground, O wise men and fools,
And each one pray to God with all his heart
That brave William Strongarm return to us 905
All safe and sound, to Rome the vast and great."
The gentle Count saw the assembled host
Pray for him —folly to further delay. **908**
He spurred his horse and slackened both the reins;
Brandished his lance with its standard of silk; 910
Struck the pagan on his vermilion targe.
He struck through the paint and varnish and wood,
Tearing through and ripping the white hauberk.
The old cuirass could not withstand the blow,
So that the lance did pass through his body 915
And came out again, with the large standard,
Just below the iron head, showing through.
Count William rode by so hard and so fast
That he wrenched the great lance from the body.
Because of his strength the pagan survived, 920
And said under his breath so none heard him:
"By Mohammad, to whom I give homage,
It is folly to blaspheme a small man
When one sees him enter a great battle.
This morning when I saw him on the turf, 925
I valued him little, him and his strength.
As well, I was so very foolhardy
When I gave him advantage over me—
No man has ever suffered so much harm."
Because he was hardy, he did not swoon. 930
Count William hastened to strike once again.

25

William was most courageous and mighty.
He struck the pagan right at his midriff
With such wrath that when he pulled out his sword
He broke the sword strap that hung at his neck, 935
And the fine gold-wrought sword stuck in the earth.
All those watching in Rome loudly cried out:
"Strike again, brave man, God guards your body!
Saint Peter, good sire, protect us all!"
Now, Count William could hear all of these words. 940
He spurred his horse, which at once shot away;
Brandished his lance, pennanted at the tip;
Struck the pagan on the hauberk he wore,
And tore through him, ripping him all open.
His old cuirass was not worth two nails then: 945
For it let the sword pass through his body,
So the iron stuck out the other side.
A lesser wound would have killed any man.
It bothered the Saracen not at all.
From his saddle-horn he took a sharp dart, 950
And hurled it at William with such great force
That it made a noise like rolling thunder.
The Count ducked very low lest he be killed.
It slashed the armor he wore on his back.
God protected him for he got no hurt. 955
"God," said the Count, "Who created Saint Loth,
Protect me that I may not wrongly die." 957

26

The Saracen knew he was sore wounded;
The dark sword stood driven into his lungs.
The blood ran in runnels down to his spurs. 960
He said softly, so no one could hear him:
"By Mohammad, whose pardon I await,
No man has dealt me so grievous a blow.
The other thing is, I have been a fool
To give him liberty to strike at me." 965
From his saddle-horn he took a sharp dart,

And hurled it at William with great anger;
It made a noise like a flying eagle.
The Count side-stepped what the felon dealt him,
Though his lion-etched sword was pierced through 970
And his old cuirass could not protect him. 971
The dart flew past him with such violence
That it sank into the sand two feet deep.
William saw this and bowed his head down low,
And called upon God, by His holy name: 975
"Glorious Father, who fashioned all the world,
And placed the earth upon a marble plinth, 977
Encircling it all with the salty sea.
You who fashioned Adam from earth and clay,
Then Eve his partner — as we surely know. 980
You gave to them the gift of paradise
And let them have the fruit of all the trees,
Save that apple tree — that was not a gift.
But they ate of it — that was a foul deed
They were expelled and cruelly punished; 985
Led to Hell, into Baratron's abyss, 986
Where they served Beelzebub and Nero. 987
Then one Easter, You made a procession:
You rode on the back of a fawn she-ass,
And all the little children followed You. 990
On Palm Sunday they made a procession;
All the priests and the clerks followed behind.
Then You lodged at Simon the Leper's house,
And then You did pardon the Magdalene,
Who broke tears upon Your feet in defeat; 995
Indeed she cried because she felt great joy.
You raised her up, holding her by the chin,
And right away forgave her many sins.
It was at that time Judas betrayed You:
He sold You — that was an evil bargain — 1000
Just thirty deniers did that rogue receive.
Then You were abandoned upon the cross.
The Jews treated You like a wretched thief:
They did not believe Your Resurrection.
You rose to the sky on Ascension Day, 1005
Where we shall gather on Redemption Day,
Where we shall gather for our judgment:

The father shall help his son not a jot,
And the priest will not rank above the clerk,
Nor the archbishop above his young page, 1010
Nor king over duke, count above server —
Nothing shall protect against treachery. 1012
You gave the Apostle the Confession; 1013
Placed Saint Peter head-down on Nero's field, 1014
And then converted Paul his companion. 1015
You guarded Jonah in the whale's belly, 1016
You preserved Saint Simeon from hunger, 1017
And saved Daniel in the den of lions. 1018
You struck down the evil Simon Magus. 1019
Moses saw the flame burning in the bush: 1020
But the bush was not consumed into coal. 1021
Since all of this is truth, which we believe,
Preserve my body from death and prison,
And keep the Saracen from killing me.
He cannot be approached for all his arms; 1025
His great crossbow hangs even by his side;
An iron mace hangs by his saddle-horn.
If He, who helped Longinus, forgets me,
I'll not conquer him — so well is he armed."
Corsolt hurled words of abuse, scorn at him: 1030
"William, you do possess a felon's heart —
Great marvel, though you seem a good champion —
Your fencing is no better than a fool's.
But now you shall not ward off my hard blows!"
Then he turned his Aragon steed around, 1035
Drew forth the great sword that hung by his side,
And struck William with such ferocity
That he slit through the nose guard and the helm,
And cut through the coif of the bright hauberk;
Sliced all his hair that grew at the front, 1040
And then cut the very tip of his nose —
That provoked much jesting for the brave man. 1042
The sword then glided off the saddle-horn
And sliced his good stallion into two halves.
So great was the blow and so violent 1045
That three hundred mail-links fell to the sand,
And the sword flew out of the felon's hand.
Then Count William leaped back up on his feet,

And unsheathed Joyous that hung at his side. 1049
He wished to strike the top of the helmet, 1050
But the pagan was so huge, large and tall,
He could not reach him, for all the world's gold.
The blow struck him on his flashing hauberk,
And three hundred mail-links fell to the sand.
His old cuirass protected well the Turk. 1055
The blow was nothing more than a spur's jab.
Corsolt hurled words of defiance at him:
"William, you do possess a felon's heart!
Your blow landed on me like a maybug."
All of Rome then cried out in one loud voice, 1060
Along with the Pope, who shook with great dread:
"Saint Peter, lord, protect now your champion.
If he dies, you will be badly reproached.
In your church, where I now presently live,
I shall not sing Mass or read the lessons." 1065

27

Now the brave and most gallant Count William
Stood fully armed upon the vast hilltop.
He watched the pagan who had lost his sword
When he cut through the backbone of his horse.
The Turk loaded his cross-bow once again, 1070
And grasped his mace and mightily raised it.
He rushed hard at William, mouth wide open;
He frothed at the mouth like a raving beast
That hounds chase after, through forest thickets. 1074
The Count saw him and raised high his round targe. 1075
The Turk struck him with such great violence
That he was quashed hard from top to bottom,
And the boss of his targe was split open;
Through that yawning, wide crack could swoop and fly
A sparrow-hawk without any nuisance. 1080
Thereupon, the mace grazed his bright helmet,
And William ducked low to escape the blow.
Rome could never be delivered by him
Without God's aid and the honored Virgin.
All of Rome, then, cried out in one loud voice. 1085

The Pope said: "Saint Peter, what do you do?
If he dies that will be an evil fate;
And in your church I shall not sing the Mass;
Where I live now, I shall live no longer."

28

Now Count William did stagger with the shock:	1090
He had received a most resounding blow.	
As well, it was a most marvelous thing	
That the Turk still sat straight upon his horse—	
Even though he was heavily bleeding.	
If he had wished, he could have knocked him down.	1095
However, he wanted to spare the horse—	
For he thought that if he could vanquish him	
He could also profit from it quite well.	
The Saracen came at him at full charge.	
When he beheld William he cried out loud:	1100
"Wretched Frank, misfortune is your true lot,	
Since you have lost a good half of your nose.	
Henceforth, you'll be Louis' prebendary,	**1103**
And all your descendents shall condemn you.	
As you know, there is no one to help you.	1105
Quite soon, I shall head back with your body,	
Since the Emir awaits me at table;	
He shall be surprised at my tardiness."	
Then he bent low over his saddle-horn,	
For he sought to rush at him right quickly;	1110
Haul him fully armed across his steed's neck.	
William saw him. Then the circumstance changed:	
He could deliver a very good blow.	
He struck the King, not caring for himself,	
On his helm of enforced iron and gold,	1115
So that jewels and gems fell to the earth;	
And he cut through the cowl of iron mail,	**1117**
Slicing to the hauberk's well-wrought lining;	
Splitting the pagan's skull a hand-width deep.	
He slumped forward across his horse's neck:	1120
Weighed by arms—he would not again sit straight.	
"God," said William, "now I've avenged my nose!	

I'll not become Louis' prebendary,
And my descendents shall not condemn me."
Then he took out his arm from his shield's straps   1125
And threw the targe to the ground — and left it:
Now no other knight could be so hardy.
If the Turk had been unhurt, hale and well,
This folly would have begun a fresh fight.
But God did not will this to go further.   1130
Then, Count William did not hold back at all:
He grasped his sword of steel with both his hands;
He struck the King, not caring for himself,
On his helm, much hardened by iron bands.
The head with the helm flew four feet away.   1135
The body tottered. The Saracen fell.
Then, Count William did not hold back at all:
The wondrous sword that had cut off his nose
He wished to gird up — but it was too long,
And so he hung it on the saddle-horn.   1140
Foot and a half too long were the stirrups:
He shortened them by a foot and a half.
Then, Count William mounted by the stirrups.
He retrieved his sword from the Saracen,
Which even yet was stuck in his body,   1145
With clotted blood smeared right across the blade.
"God," said William, "how greatly I thank You
For this stallion that I have won today.
I would not sell it for Montpellier's gold,   **1149**
Nor for all of the gold I can covet."   1150
All those in Rome did not tarry further.
Now the Pope was the first to come outside
And kissed him before he unlaced his helm.
Count Bertrand, his nephew, came out weeping,
Along with Guiélin and brave Gautier —   1155
They did not know such dread in all their days.
"Uncle," said Bertrand, "are you safe and sound?"
"Yes," said he, "by God's grace who is above.
My nose has now been shortened a little —
But I know well my name will be lengthened!"   1160
Right then the Count baptized himself again:
"Henceforth, all those who love and cherish me,
The Franks and men of Berry, shall call me

The gallant, brave warrior, William Shortnose."
Thenceforth, he never again changed his name. 1165
They did not tarry till they reached the church;
Those who held his stirrups were filled with joy.
That night they gave a feast for the brave knight,
Which lasted all night till the light of day—
For they had so many things to speak of. 1170
Then Bertrand loudly cried out: "Knights to arms!
Since my uncle has conquered in the field,
Against the strongest, deemed invincible—
It's fitting we fight those considered weak.
Uncle William rest now and take your ease, 1175
For you have undergone a hard ordeal."
William heard him and laughed in amusement:
"Ah Bertrand, now you are annoying me!
And you do not have to contradict me—
By the Apostle to whom pilgrims pray, **1180**
By Montpellier's gold, I will not give up
Being right at the front of the foremost rank
And striking with the steel of my broadsword."
When the men of Rome heard him speak these words
The most cowardly became brave and brisk. 1185
Thenceforth, the felons were ever on guard,
And no more took their ease and lazed about,
For the men of Rome now went fully armed.

29

Galafrez the King came out of his tent;
He was dressed and fitted most like a king. 1190
He said to his men: "I lost completely
When Corsolt was defeated by that man.
The God in whom they trust merits belief.
Come now, and quickly dismantle my tent.
Let us all flee. What are we waiting for? 1195
For if the men of Rome see our plight
No man in our army shall escape."
They responded: "We shall heed this counsel."
And then fourteen trumpets sounded as one;
The army mounted and began to flee. 1200

William heard this great tumult and uproar.
He said to his men: "We have heard enough!
The pagans are fleeing—the wretched fiends—
Let's after them, by God, and King Jesus!"
The men of Rome gave voice to a loud cry; 1205
And William was at the very forefront—
The noble Count certainly proved his worth.
He pricked at Alion with his sharp spurs:
It reared up, though it was used to great pain—
But its new rider sat light upon it. 1210
Between the two hills they chased the pagans. **1211**
Then there was seen combat most courageous:
Many feet, heads and chests were hacked away!
Now Count Bertrand disposed himself most well:
After hurling his lance, he drew his sword. 1215
Those whom he attacked were rent to the breast;
Their bright hauberks were no better than straw.
He took and gave back a great many blows.
Guiélin also struck many great blows,
Along with Gautier, who was from Toulouse. 1220
And of them all, William was the boldest.
Now King Galafrez looked all around him.
William struck hard the shield slung on his neck.
And when King Galafrez saw him do this,
He called upon Mohammad and Cahut: 1225
"Lord Mohammad, what evil befalls me!
If it be your will, show your great power
So that I may seize and destroy William."
With sharpened spurs he jabbed at his war-horse,
But Count William stood still and showed no fright. 1230
They both struck hard at the top of the shields,
Which cracked and split all around the bosses.
Their bright hauberks were all shredded and torn,
And their flanks now felt the cut of iron.
God helped William the most redoubtable, 1235
As did Saint Peter whose champion he was.
Now he did not stand and wait for the King:
The noble Count gave him such a great blow,
He lost his footing in both his stirrups.
The horse bent down low when it felt the blow; 1240
And then the King was tossed upon the ground.

The point of his helm struck upon the earth
With such force that both the laces broke off.
Then, Count William stood right on top of him,
And drew out his sword made of sharpest steel   1245
To strike off the head right from the body—
Then God showed a miracle, and His might:
For suffering, afflicted prisoners
Were that very day released from prison.

30

Count William was a most valorous knight.   1250
He saw the King tumble down before him;
If he wished he could have sliced off his head.
But he cried out for mercy and pity:
"Brave knight, slay me not, as you are William:
Take me alive, and profit much by it.   1255
You shall have back the brave, rich King Guaifier,
Along with his daughter and noble wife,
And thirty thousand wretched prisoners
Who, if I die now, shall all lose their heads."
"By Saint Denis," said the fiery-faced Count,   1260
"For such a thing you surely shall be spared."
Now, Count William sat firm in the stirrups;
The King yielded his costly sword of steel.
Right away he led the King to the Pope,
And thirteen hundred other prisoners.   1265
When the Saracens, those faithless wretches,
Saw the great abasement of their true lord,
They all fled by any road or pathway;
They tarried not, even at the Tiber,
Where sat all their ships that they most needed.   1270
They boarded; sailed down the sandy river.
And then Count William returned to the rear.
They disarmed the King 'neath an olive tree.
The noble Count addressed these words to him:
"O good King, in the name of God, the just,   1275
How shall we get back the lost prisoners,
Who lie tied and fettered in your barges?"
The King responded: "You speak in folly,

For by the Cross which the pilgrims invoke,
You shall not receive a single denier   1280
Before I am first washed and then baptized,
Since Mohammad no longer can aid me."
"God," said William, "shall show you much kindness!"
Nor did the Pope much tarry or linger.
Quickly he prepared and readied the fonts,   1285
And then he washed and baptized the good King.
His godfathers were William the gallant,
Guiélin and the most courteous Gautier,
As well as over thirty gallant knights,
All of whom were the foremost, the bravest.   1290
But he did not agree to change his name;
He was baptized Christian by his own name.
They asked for water, and sat down to eat.
Now when they had eaten and drank their fill,
Count William rose up and got to his feet: 1295
"O gentle King, by God who is most just,
Most noble godson, come forth. Show yourself.
How shall we get back the lost prisoners
Who lie tied and fettered in your barges?"
The King replied: "I must think about it;   1300
For if the Saracens and pagans learn
That I have come to be washed and baptized,
Most quickly shall they have me skinned alive
And worth no more than a single denier.
Rather despoil me of all my clothing,   1305
Put me on a wretched beast of burden,
And let me be led away by three knights
Close to the Tiber, so I may cry out.
But meanwhile, have all your men stand ready
Beneath this wall, in this small olive grove.   1310
If the Saracens then bestir themselves
And seek to help me and even save me,
Stand ready to bring them down with lances."
"God," said William, "by Your most kind mercy
We've such a convert among bread-eaters."   1315
Right away they heeded his good advice;
But they did not beat him — this they spared him:
They smeared him with the blood of a greyhound.   1318
By the Tiber they did not tarry long.

Then King Galafrez began to cry out, 1320
Loudly shouting: "Lord Champion, my nephew!
O son of a baron, rescue me now
By releasing the wretched prisoners.
Know this: in this way shall I be set free!"
Champion then said: "Mohammad aids you well, 1325
In that an exchange shall save your body."
Thereat, they hauled the barge right to the shore
And then took out the wretched prisoners,
Who had been soundly thrashed by the pagans,
Following their base defeat and capture. 1330
Not one among them was not all bloodied
About the waist, shoulders, back, or the head.
Out of pity brave-hearted William wept.

31

When the wretched emerged from the barges,
Not one was without a blood-spattered face, 1335
And blood covered their shoulders and their chests.
Out of pity William Strongarm did weep.
He saw the Pope and asked him for advice:
"Sire," he said, "by God who is spirit,
So many noblemen are all naked. 1340
Let us give them clothing, mantles and capes,
And let Rome give gold and silver to all
That they may return, each one to his home."
The Pope said: "Noble, honorable man,
To honor them, we shall show great largesse. 1345
Your council is wise; let it be followed."
They did not stop until they had reached Rome.
For the captives, they unlocked the coffers,
And gave them all clothing, mantles and capes,
Along with gold and silver for each man 1350
That they may return, each one to his home.

32

When all the captives had returned to Rome,
Count William sat down upon a stone step.

Then the great King Guaifier came up to him
And at once threw himself down at his feet. 1355
"Noble lord, you have helped me in my need,
Delivering me from my enemies,
As I lay captive and bound in their land,
No more to see my own realms and fiefdoms.
Now I have a daughter most beautiful; 1360
Happy would I be to give her to you,
If you would take and hold her as your wife.
I shall also give you half of my land
That you may be my own heir past my death."
The Count replied: "I must seek some advice." 1365
Then he saw the Pope and took him aside:
"Lord," he said, "should I take her as my wife?"
"Yes, noble lord, happily and freely.
You are unwed and need to have some land." **1369**
The Count responded: "Good. I shall accept." 1370
They came and presented him his betrothed —
No man of flesh, no pilgrim or palmer, **1372**
Who has oft journeyed on horse or on foot,
Has ever seen a more beautiful maid.
Now, William the gallant went to wed her — 1375
But an unseen obstacle delayed him —
As you shall soon learn, before the sun sets. **1377**

33

Would you like to hear of her great beauty?
No man of flesh, though he be well-traveled,
Shall have known a more beautiful maiden. 1380
Now, William Shortnose was to marry her,
But an unseen obstacle delayed him,
As you shall learn, before evening draws nigh.
Two messengers arrived, riding pell-mell:
They came from France. They and all their horses 1385
Were weak from exhaustion and great fatigue.
They eagerly came, sought out good William.
And then they found the Count inside the church —
He was just about to wed the young maid,
With the Pope, most noble and valiant, 1390

In full vestments ready to sing the Mass—
He held the ring to make the maid his wife.
They dashed in and threw themselves at his feet:
"Mercy, lord William, by kind charity!
Remember and think of Louis somewhat,   1395
For Charles is dead, the most gentle and brave.
To Louis has come a great heritage,
And traitors now want to give him the boot,
For they do wish to crown another king—
The son of Richard, of Rouen city.   1400
All the land is wracked by sorrow and grief.
O gentle lord, there is no help but you."
William heard them and hung his head down low.
He saw the Pope and turned to him to say:
"Lord," said he, "what counsel can you give me?"   1405
The Pope said: "That which shall glorify God!
Such counsel I give to all those who ask.
Now this I shall ask of you as penance:
That you go and succor your lord Louis.
Grievous it would be if he were chased off."   1410
The Count replied: "It shall be as you ask,
For your counsel can never be refused."
Count William then kissed that fair-faced maiden,
Who returned his kiss; her tears did not cease.
In this way were these two separated.   1415
In all their lives, they did not meet again.   **1416**
"Sire William," said the most gallant Pope,
"You must rightly now return to sweet France.
But Emir Galafrez shall remain here,
And he shall watch over Rome in your name."   1420
The Count responded: "You speak in folly:
Never shall I be accused of treason—
Ever shall I be on guard against it."
"Sire William," said the most gallant Pope,
"You must rightly now return to sweet France,   1425
And you shall take with you your thousand knights.
Thirty mules laden with gold and silver:
You shall carry away what you have won."
The Count replied: "For that I must thank you."

34

One Sunday, fourteen days after Easter,	1430
Gallant Count William Strongarm was in Rome;	
He was just about to wed a young maid—	
Quickly had he forgotten Orable—	**1433**
When suddenly heralds arrived from France,	
Who were the bearers of some painful news:	1435
That the Emperor Charlemagne was dead,	
And all the fiefdoms now fell to Louis.	
But traitors—whose bodies may God well rot—	
Wanted Richard of Rouen the Bearded's	
Son to be made king before the barons.	1440
Then, William Strongarm wept with compassion.	
He sought leave of the Pope who was so wise;	
And he gave to him a thousand armed knights,	
Thirty beasts laden with gold and silver.	
At his leaving all of the nobles wept.	1445
Thus did the Count leave; nothing hindered him.	
He crossed over Montjeu with great hardships.	
I cannot tell you of all his journey.	
Till Brie they did not tarry or linger.	

35

And thus traveled Marquis William Shortnose.	1450
I cannot tell you of all his journey.	
Right to Brie he traveled without respite.	
Now on his journey he met a pilgrim:	
Sash on his neck; ashen staff in his fist;	1454
No one had seen a more sprightly pilgrim;	1455
All white was his beard like April flowers.	
When William saw him, he at once called out:	
"Whence come you, brother?"—"Saint Martin of Tours."	1458
"Do you have any news to give to us?"	
"Yes noble lord, about little Louis.	1460
Charlemagne is dead, King of Saint Denis;	
And now all the realm belongs to Louis.	
The traitors—all of whom may God condemn—	
Now seek white-haired Richard of Rouen's son	

To be king and hold France in governance. 1465
But one noble abbot — may God bless him —
Inside a crypt at Saint Martin's Abbey,
Has taken shelter along with the lad;
Those that guarded them have all been murdered.
O God help us!" said the worthy pilgrim. 1470
"Where are all the noble and valiant knights?
The offspring of Aimeri, the gallant?
For they were the great support of their lord.
By that cross upon which God's body hung,
If I be the man that succors Louis, 1475
I shall deal with these traitors severely;
They had no cause to betray their liege lord." **1477**
Hearing him, William let out a loud laugh.
He called out to Bertrand and said to him:
"Have you ever heard a nobler pilgrim? 1480
If he were the man to succor Louis,
The felons would not have hatched such a plot."
Ten ounces of gold he gave the pilgrim
Who, much pleased, took his leave and went his way.
And William took to his path once again. 1485
Happy is the man who has many friends!
William turned and looked at the road behind.
He saw one hundred forty knights riding,
With flashing arms, mounted on prized horses.
Dark Gualdin, the marquis, was leading them; 1490
Riding with him was Savaris the brave.
Now, both were nephews of Marquis William.
They had come to France to rescue Louis.
But what a surprise awaited them all.
They embraced, for they were nephews and friends. 1495
The high-born Abbot had no doubt they'd come —
He who had guarded the little Louis.
He had guarded and protected him well,
And hid him from the kin of Alori.
It was on the third day that help arrived. 1500

36

Thus traveled William the gallant warrior.
Together with him were twelve hundred knights.

To these men he made a declaration,
And they rushed to him on charger and steed;
At once he told them without much delay 1505
Not to spare their horses in any way,
Though a steed or charger come to perish.
"An evil event is soon to begin;
And in time I shall come to know fully
Who is to be the rightful king of France. 1510
By the Apostle to whom pilgrims pray,
That man must show himself noble and brave,
On whose head I shall come to place the crown,
And whose brain shall not go down to his feet!" **1514**
The Romans said: "This man has a brave heart. 1515
Let God heap hardships on those who fail him!"
I cannot recall all their daily deeds.
At Tours they took care not to linger long.
They proceeded with the greatest caution:
A thousand knights set up four ambuscades. 1520
Now, two hundred armed knights rode with William.
They all wore their shining double hauberks.
Beneath their hoods they wore well-laced green helms.
Their hard, bright swords were girded for the fray.
Following behind were doughty riders, 1525
With their strong long shields and sharpest lances.
William held back these riders in reserve.
When they reached the gates, they did not tarry;
At once they called out to the gatekeeper:
"Open the gate. And do not make us wait! 1530
We have come to lend aid to Duke Richard.
Today in church his son shall be crowned king.
Thus have the Franks deemed it fitting and right."
Hearing them, the gatekeeper was wrathful.
He invoked God, the Father of justice: 1535
"Saint Mary," said the gentle gatekeeper,
"Louis, my lord, how great is your distress!
If He who judges all was not involved,
You would not leave without being torn apart.
O God, send aid," said the brave gatekeeper. 1540
"Where have the noble and gallant knights gone?
Brave offspring of Aimeri the warrior?
Those who were the brace of their rightful lord?"

And he said to William: "Come not inside.
Many vile villains are but now within.   1545
I do not want you to boost their number.
Great marvel that the earth yet sustains you.
It pleases the splendid King of Heaven
That earth does not collapse beneath your feet,
And Louis return to his rightful fief!   1550
The world shall avenge all evil people."
Hearing all these words William was right glad.
He said to Bertrand: "Listen, lord nephew.
Have you ever heard gatekeepers speak thus?
If we showed him the depths of our hearts,   1555
He would be most useful to us today."

37

"Friend, gentle brother," said gallant William,
"Foolishly you have kept me from your house.
But if you knew which land I was born in,
And of which people and which family.   1560
I dare say if I were to tell you this,
Freely, gladly would you open the gates."
At this, the gatekeeper sprang to his feet.
He opened the window so to see him.
"Most gentle lord, if I may be so bold,   1565
I would like to ask from which land you come.
Who are your people? Which your family?"
"Indeed," said William, "Hear now the full truth.
For dread of no man shall I hide my name:
Hark, I am William of Narbonne-on-sea."   1570
Then said the gatekeeper: "Now God be praised!
Lord William, it is just as you have said:
Your parentage can never be hidden.
The evil Richard has entered within,
Together with seven hundred armed knights.   1575
Most gentle lord, you have but a few men,
And you cannot last long against their force."
Then William said to him: "We have enough.
Deployed and waiting are four ambuscades
Of a thousand knights, all armed and eager;   1580

With me are two hundred, all well equipped;
Beneath their clothes they wear shining hauberks;
Beneath their hoods they have jeweled, green helms;
Behind them are riders in great numbers;
And if need be we can call upon them." 1585
"May God be praised," said the gatekeeper then.
"Now if you were to ask for my council,
At once abandon the four ambuscades;
Send runners to bring men secretly back.
The traitors are all well-ensconced within. 1590
Why search all over when they are all here?
And on this day, in truth, draw them all out,
Before the morn of the next day rises,
And thus seal their fate, as you would most want.
A man who wants to act in the same way 1595
Must be savage as a boar in the woods." **1596**
At these words, William hung his head down low.
He said to Bertrand: "Good nephew, hear me:
Have you ever heard gatekeepers speak thus?"

38

Now when the gatekeeper had heard the news 1600
From gallant William, whose courage shone forth,
He turned his head around to the palace.
He took a glove, held it in his right fist, **1603**
And cried out in a most strong and fine voice:
"I defy you Richard, you and your land. 1605
I shall be in your service no longer,
For you have sought and committed treason.
Thus it is right and just that you perish."
And the gate was fast opened for William,
And just as fast shut and bolted again. 1610
Then William entered with his host of men.
In a lowered voice, the gatekeeper said:
"Brave and noble knight, go and get revenge
From traitors that revolted against you."
William heard him and bowed his head down low. 1615
Then quickly he summoned a mounted knight:
"Go and speak to Lord Gautier of Tudèle,

Then to Guarin of Rome — on my behalf —
That all gates have been opened up for me.
Those who wish to conquer and win booty   1620
Must come now, without noise or show of joy."
The mounted knight rushed off without delay.
Thus all the knights forsook their ambuscades;
They entered the gates that opened for them.
Those inside looked from their walls and windows;   1625
They thought that these were men they had sent for.
But on that day they got other tidings,
Which would be painful and bitter for them.

39

Then Count William said to the gatekeeper:
"Friend, gentle brother, will you council me?   1630
I have many men who need to be lodged?"
"By God's name, lord, I know not what to say,
For there is no vault or crypt or cellar
Which is not now full of horses and men.
And there are knights lodged in all of the homes.   1635
You have the power to convince these men
To don their armor and seize their weapons.
And he who now does not show a good heart
Shall risk no more than have his head cut off!"
Now William said, "You have counseled me well,   1640
By Saint Denis. And I ask for no more.
You shall be guard and gatekeeper no more:
You shall be chief among my counselors."
Then he called Bertrand: "Listen, lord nephew,
Have you ever heard gatekeepers speak thus?   1645
Arm him now like a solemnly sworn knight."
Bertrand replied: "Well lord, it shall be done."
He looked him up and down from head to toe;
He was noble, handsome, well-proportioned.   **1649**
He was armed in the manner of all knights: 1650
With a strong hauberk, a helmet of steel,
With a marvelous sword and a sharp lance,
With a horse, a charger, and a squire,
A palfrey, a mule, a beast of burden —

He was well recompensed for his service! 1655
And then Count William summoned forth Gautier
The Toulousean, as I've heard him called,
The son of his sister, a noble knight:
"Now this gate that looks out towards Poitiers
Hold it for me, O noble lady's son; 1660
You shall have with you twenty gallant knights.
Let no man leave who walks beneath the sky;
No clerk nor priest, though he know how to pray; **1663**
But that he shall have all his limbs hacked off."
He replied: "Well, lord, glad shall I do this." 1665

40

And then Count William Shortnose, the Marquis
Right quickly summoned Seier of Plessis:
"By the gate that opens towards Paris,
Go there and take up your post, noble knight,
And take with you some twenty gallant knights. 1670
Guard the gate well and let no mother's son
Issue forth without being cut down and killed."
And he said: "It shall be done as you say."
There was no rampart or gate or postern
Where the Count did not place his gallant knights. 1675
Right up to the church he went as he pleased.
Then he dismounted upon the flagstones
And went inside the church, crossing himself.
On the marble, before the crucifix,
Behold, William the Marquis then did kneel, 1680
And prayed to God, who was put on the cross,
That He deliver his liege lord Louis.
And then Gautier a clerk came up to him —
Quickly he recognized Marquis William.
He placed his finger upon his shoulder 1684
So that the Count would know of his presence.
The Count got to his feet and showed his face:
"What do you want, brother? Careful! Don't lie!"
The other said: "I overheard you say:
That you have come now to rescue Louis; 1690
Shut are all the doors of Saint Martin's Church.

Inside are twenty-five clerks and canons,
Bishops and abbots of very high rank,
Who have come out of avarice and greed.
Today is Louis disinherited,   1695
If God and you do not come to his aid.
Cut off all their heads, by God, I pray you!
I shall bear the sin of blood in the church —
For they are all traitors and vile wretches."
When William heard his words, he laughed out loud: 1700
"Happy the day when such a clerk was born!
Now, where can I find my liege lord Louis?"
"In the name of God, sire," said the clerk,
I'll show you, if God wills, and I yet live."
They did not rest till they had reached the church.   1705
Quietly they went down into the crypt,
Where they found their worthy liege lord Louis.
Then the gentle clerk took him by the hand:
"Son of a good king, do not be afraid;
By the grace of God, you have many friends,   1710
Who shall never let this morning arise.
For behold Marquis William has now come
Together with twelve hundred gallant knights.
He came seeking you in the church below.
There is no rampart or gate or postern   1715
Where he has not placed his most gallant knights."
Louis heard this news; he was filled with joy.
At once he was whisked away to the church.
The noble Abbot said these words to him:
"Son of a good king, do not be afraid.   1720
Behold William has pledged you all his faith.
Fall at his feet and beg for his mercy."
The lad replied: "It shall be as you wish."

41

The noble abbot said to him first off:
"Noble warrior's son, do not be afraid;   1725
Behold William. Go and fall at his feet."
The lad said: "Glad shall I do this, good sir."
Then before the Count he went and knelt down,

And straightaway he clutched and kissed his feet,
By his well-fitting boots he embraced him. 1730
Gallant William did not recognize him,
Because the light in the church was but dim:
"Rise up, lad." Thus spoke the most esteemed Count.
"No man, made by God, has wronged me so much
That if he come and fall down at my feet, 1735
That I shall not forgive him most freely."
Then the abbot, who spoke for Louis, said:
"In God's name, lord, no more shall I hide this—
It is Louis, Charlemagne the bold's son.
Today he shall be killed and cut to bits, 1740
If God and you do not come to his aid."
At this, William ran to hug the good lad.
Bodily he picked him up straightaway.
"In the name of God, lad, that man was wrong
Who told you to come and fall at my feet, 1745
For I, of all men, must come to your aid."
Quickly he summoned his most noble knights:
"I would like you to pronounce a judgment.
From the time a man is tonsured in church,
And he only lives to read the Psalter, 1750
Is he right to commit treason for pay?"
"No, he is not right, good lord," said the knights.
"And if he does, what shall be his reward?"
"He should be hanged like any common thief!"
The Count replied: "You have counseled me well, 1755
By Saint Denis, and I ask for no more.
God's divine order must not be abased— **1757**
Therefore they shall all pay enormously!"

42

In this way, Count William the most gallant
Heard the judgment of the gathered barons. 1760
Then to the chancel he went in all haste.
There he found the bishops and the abbots,
And the clerks who were false to their true lord.
He snatched away the crosiers from their hands,
And gave them to Louis his rightful lord. 1765

Then the brave Count embraced him with his arms,
And did kiss the lad four times on his face. **1767**
Now, Count William let nothing hinder him:
And to the chancel he went in all haste,
Where he found the bishop and the abbots. 1770
To do no sin, they did not touch their arms,
But took staffs, fell upon them, and beat them;
They hounded them out; dragged them from the church,
And then dispatched all the eighty devils.
He who commits treason against his lord 1775
Should ever be dealt with in this manner. **1776**

43

Now Count William was the most chivalrous.
He turned and said to Louis his liege lord:
"Sire," said he, "do listen to my plea;
I would that we send out a messenger 1780
To Acelin on your behalf, and say:
Return to Louis your lord; make amends."
Louis said: "Sir, we give our consent."
Then he summoned Aliaume the baron:
"Now go and speak to Acelin the proud, 1785
To come to Louis his lord; make amends
Very quickly, for he yearns to see him."
Aliaume replied, "Shall I go alone?"
"Yes, brave brother, with a staff in your hand." **1789**
"And if he asks me how much force we have?" 1790
"Then tell him we have forty companions. **1791**
And if he firmly refuses to come,
Say to him, before all his companions,
That before dusk he shall be put to shame,
Which all Avalon's gold will not erase." 1795
Aliaume said: "I shall do as you wish,
By that Apostle killed on Nero's field,
And boldly take this message unafraid."
He then mounted a mule from Aragon,
And went through the streets, spurring on the beast; 1800
He did not stop till he came to the house.
He found Acelin with his companions.

He then called out to him in a loud voice:
"Lord Acelin, most noble and gentle,
Do you know you are summoned by William 1805
The brave, the Strongarm, the lion-hearted?
Return to Louis your lord; make amends
Very quickly, for he yearns to see you."
Hearing this, Acelin hung low his chin.
"Friend," said he, "I grasp your words; but tell me 1810
How many companions has your uncle?"
"By God's name, sire, he has thirty knights."
Acelin said: "May God be exalted!
Go and tell William the most courageous
To agree and do what the others want. 1815
Tell him that he should give the crown to me.
France shall be led to ruin by this boy: **1817**
I value Louis no more than a bud!
Count William is most marvelously brave,
And yet he has no land or rich holdings. 1820
But I shall provide him with all of this;
A region he shall rule for his delight;
Ten mules laden with fine gold and mangons. **1823**
Indeed, he shall be a very rich man."
"Truly," said Aliaume, "You speak vainly. 1825
He can't be bought by all Avalon's gold.
He summons you still. Why should I hide this?
One cruel thing we have not spoken of:
If you resolutely refuse to come
Before dusk you shall be put to great shame, 1830
Which all the world's goodness will not erase."
Acelin said: "May God be exalted!
Since I bear him neither love nor hatred.
I defy him. Go, tell him this from me."
Aliaume replied: "I have heard your words. 1835
And on my part I say the same to you:
I defy you, as your barons all hear."

44

Acelin was very proud and doughty;
He looked at Aliaume, from head to foot;

He saw that he was tall and most handsome: 1840
He could see that he was a noble knight.
"Friend, gentle brother, you are ill-informed,
You, who have disgraced me before my knights.
I care not a denier for your uncle.
Since I bear him neither ill-will or love, 1845
I challenge him to come, cut off my head:
Today I shall tear him from limb-to-limb,
For I have with me seven hundred knights,
And four counts who are all men of valor:
They shall not blame me for losing some limbs! 1850
If you had not come as a messenger,
I would even now strike off your proud head,
And destroy, annihilate your body!"
Aliaume said: "Cursed be he who dreads you!"
Then he left the court without taking leave. 1855
Straightaway, Acelin prepared his men.
The brave Aliaume mounted his charger,
And through the streets he went with all due speed.
He came to William the bold warrior.
He asked him: "How did you acquit yourself?" 1860
"In God's name, sire, not with amity,
For he deems Louis not as his liege lord.
When I told him the number of your knights,
Right away he became most menacing;
He challenged you to come, cut off his head. 1865
If I had not gone as a messenger,
Straightaway he would have cut off my limbs,
Burnt them and thrown them into the water."
Hearing these words, William grew most angry.
He summoned forth his men from their lodgings. 1870
He piled up all the arms into a heap—
And those who did not take them willingly
Ventured nothing but the loss of their heads.
Seeing this, the burghers began to flee;
But the Count stopped them and had them all bound. 1875
The traitors—upon whom God heaped great shame—
Those who had first begun this evil plot,
Sought to flee by the speed of their good steeds.
They spurred on hard until they reached the gates,
But the most hostile gatekeepers met them: 1880

Then was hard justice unleashed upon them —
No more did they fret about waging war,
And none bore them in their prayers or thoughts.
Thereupon, Count William spurred hard away
To the house of the brave burgher Hungier.   1885
He found Acelin seated on the steps—
But the felon was so grim and so proud
That he did not deign to stand up for him.
When William saw him, he was filled with rage.
But he was alone; the others many.   1890
Then did he sound his horn, most loud and high—   **1891**
You should have seen all the knights come rushing!
Leading them all were Bertrand and Gautier,
And they brought with them a thousand armed knights.
Then was seen a battle hard and brutal: 1895
How the lances splintered; bucklers shattered!
How the hauberks tore; chain-mail unraveled!
When the traitors launched a ruthless assault,
William's men also fought very bravely.
The traitors learned all their strength was useless: 1900
And they dropped their shining blades at their feet
And with joined hands they pleaded for mercy.
The Count gathered them all and had them bound.
Acelin, on his part, fled with all haste;
Count William chased right after him swiftly   1905
And hurled after him a bitter reproach:
"Sire Acelin, return and come back
So you may have your crowning in the church.
And what a crowning we shall give to you:
Your brains shall lie spattered all at your feet!"   **1910**

45

Now Count William, the bravest of all men,
Saw Acelin; said these hard words to him:
"Traitor! Brigand! God will now destroy you!
Why did you show your true lord such disgrace?
Richard, your father, shall never be crowned."   1915
And there came Bertrand with his bright, long sword.
Seeing him, William spoke these grim, hard words:

"Good nephew," he said, "We ask your counsel
For this traitor. How shall we now kill him?"
And then said Bertrand, "Why ask, good uncle? 1920
Let us put such a crown upon his head
That all his brains shall spill out from his mouth!"
He then stepped forth, his broadsword in his hand,
To strike him down, watched by a hundred men.
Then, Count William, his uncle, said to him: 1925
"Good nephew," he said, "do not yet touch him.
It does not please God, who made all the world,
That he die by the hand of a brave man!
I shall kill him in so shameful a way
That all his heirs shall suffer great reproach." 1930

46

Now, Count William was a most gallant knight:
Severe was he to those who were haughty,
Like a leopard ready to eat up men.
He did not deign to strike him with his arms. **1934**
In a vine arbor he saw a sharp stake, 1935
And he strode forth and quickly snatched it up.
He struck foul Acelin on the forehead,
And blood and brains gushed forth down to his feet:
And then right there he died, without delay.
"Montjoie!" he cried, "Saint Denis has helped me 1940
Avenge Louis, the true and rightful king!"
Then, Count William began to spur away;
He did not stop until he reached the church.
And there he bowed to Louis, his true lord:
He ran up and embraced him in his arms. 1945
"Ah, young lord, who now feels sorry for you?
I have avenged you before Richard's son —
No more has he any need to wage war;
No man shall remember him in prayer."
"God has shown us great mercy," said the lad. 1950
If I can now pay his father in kind,
I shall be filled with joy and elation."
"O God," said William, "Tell me where is he?"
It happened that he was found in the church.

The Crowning of Louis

The Count rushed away at a great gallop,   1955
And some eighty knights rushed right after him.
He found Richard leaning on the altar.
He found no peace although he was in church.
With his strong hand he grabbed him by the hair,
And dragged him low until he kissed the ground.   1960
Then he dealt him a blow right at the nape.
So that he fell at his feet in a daze.
And right quickly he hacked off all his limbs,
So that he possessed neither hands nor feet.
Then, looking at him, William reproached him: 1965
"Leave, wretch! God has given you your reward!"
Then he asked for scissors and cropped his head.   **1967**
Thus he lay, all stretched out on the marble.
Then he exclaimed, in front of all the knights:
"Thus is justice given to a traitor   1970
Who betrays and deceives his rightful lord."
But all the barons and all the counts prayed
For peace between both Richard and William;
He was punished enough by his son's death.
Then was peace made before he left the church: 1975
They kissed each other before many knights.   **1976**
But this accord was not worth one denier,
For they then sought to kill noble William
With a shining knife, in a dense forest—
But God would not let this happen to him.   1980
Count William did not linger or tarry.
He called upon the good Abbot Gautier:
"I must go now to the realm of Poitiers;
So many traitors are harbored out there.
But, God willing, I shall flush them all out.   1985
My rightful liege lord I must leave to you.
Guard him well. And if he seeks amusement
Let him take with him some one hundred knights.
By the Apostle to whom pilgrims pray,
If upon my return I come to find   1990
That Louis was placed in hardship by you,
Your holy orders shall not be enough
To keep me from ripping you limb-to-limb!"   **1993**
The Abbot replied: "You need not say that.
He shall be watched like our sacred church."   1995

Now, Count William was a most gallant knight.
Across the land he sent letters of writ,
Summoning forth all the brave baron knights.
Before fifteen days had passed completely,
Some fifteen thousand knights came and gathered. 2000
All those who assembled left for Poitiers.
And for William, the following three years,
Not a day passed, no matter how festive,
That he did not lace up his brown helmet,
Girded his sword; sat armed upon his horse. 2005
He kept no holy days, on which one prays,
Nor yet Christmas, celebrated by all.
But armed, girded in his hauberk he sat.
Indeed, this brave knight endured great torment
To aid and assist and sustain his lord. 2010

47

Now, for three years did William the gallant
Stay in Poitou, so to conquer the land.
Not one day passed, no matter how solemn —
Neither Easter Day, nor yet Christmas Day,
Nor All Saints' Day, celebrated by all — 2015
When he did not lace up his brown helmet,
Girded his sword; sat armed upon his horse.
Indeed, this young man endured great torment
To protect and defend his rightful lord.

48

Then Count William, who was noble-hearted, 2020
Proceeded to Bordeaux by the Gironde,
And there he vanquished strong King Amarmonde,
Who then received the crown in Louis' name,
Along with fiefs that were great and most vast.

49

Then Count William, who was noble-hearted 2025
Wended his way back along Pierelarge.

Then he vanquished Dagobert of Carthage,
Who then gave his land to Louis the wise,
Along with fiefs that were great and most vast.

50

Thereafter, Count William who was most wise, 2030
Took the path that led him to Annadore.
And then one morning he attacked Saint Giles;
He did take that city without delay.
But he did one thing that pleased Jesus most:
He made sure that the church was not despoiled. 2035
There he captured Julian, ward of the land. **2036**
Hostages were given, as pleased the Count
To guarantee the peace now established.
Then Count William summoned all his people
And told them something that pleased all of them: 2040
"Bind up your armor, gentle, honored men;
Each one may return to his own country;
Each one to his wife, those who are married."

51

Then, Count William Shortnose, the brave warrior,
Hastily did ride off towards sweet France. 2045
But he left most of his knights at Poitou,
Who filled the fortresses and the castles.
Two hundred well-armed men he kept with him.
Thus he traversed the whole of Brittany,
Not halting till he reached Mont-Saint-Michel. 2050
There he stayed two days and left on the third.
He headed back by way of Cotentin.
I need not tell you all about those days.
He did not tarry till he reached Rouen.
The Count took lodging in the main district. 2055
But he showed thoughtlessness about one thing:
He was not afraid to pass and ride through
The territory of old Duke Richard,
Whose own son he had slain with a great stake.
But the gentle knight put his trust and hope 2060

In the accord of peace struck between them.
But this accord was not worth one denier,
For they sought to kill and mutilate him.
"Truly," said Richard, "I am full of rage,
For that man is passing through my own land 2065
Who has taken my eldest heir from me,
Who no more shall sit and rule over land.
By the Apostle to whom pilgrims pray,
He shall surely come to harm ere he leaves."
"In the name of God, sire," said his knights, 2070
"Yet we cannot touch him in this city,
For all the burghers shall come to his aid;
It is not good to start an uprising."
And Richard replied: "I am most angry.
I shall inform him with great amity 2075
That I will join him and ride to sweet France.
We shall be sixteen men, very well armed.
If we can draw away his companions,
Each one of us shall have a sharp steel knife.
Soon shall he be murdered, mutilated." 2080
Right quickly fifteen knights promised him aid.
Better that they had left him all alone
For, when put to the test, they reaped disgrace.
God! The brave-faced Count suspected nothing!
When morning arose, he mounted his horse, 2085
And rode to Lyons, a vast rich forest.
In a moor they dismounted; went by foot,
And the peasants gave them something to eat.
When the brave knights had all eaten their fill,
Some fell asleep, overcome by fatigue. 2090
Seeing his men, good William took pity.
He called for his arms to equip himself;
They rushed to bring him these quickly enough.
He donned his hauberk, laced his steel helmet,
Sheathed his sword, with its pommel of worked gold. **2095**
Then they led Alion, his horse to him
And the Count mounted by the left stirrup;
Then he hung his strapped long shield on his neck;
Grasped in his fist a solid and sharp lance,
To which fifteen nails fixed firm his standard. 2100
And he took with him no more than two knights;

By the river's side they amused themselves.
Then Duke Richard the Old came into sight,
For whom they had been waiting the whole day.
He had with him some fifteen hardy knights.　　　　　2105
Seeing this, William grew very fretful.

52

Count William was riding, hard by a hill,
When Duke Richard the Red came into sight;
He had with him some fifteen companions.
Seeing this, William was very afraid.　　　　　2110
Thereat, he turned to his two gallant knights,
And quietly spoke and reasoned with them:
"Barons, say, what did we set out to do?
Duke Richard the Red is coming to us.
He hates me for taking his great treasure:　　　　　2115
I did slay his son, and that he well knows.
However, both of us were reconciled
By the peace deal reached in the church at Tours."
They replied: "Why are you afraid of him?
Spur your horse out to him, just by the bridge.　　　　　2120
Greet him with amity and affection.
If all your words and reasons come to naught,
Use your long shield adorned with a lion.
We shall not fault you for all the world's gold."
William replied, "Barons, I do thank you."　　　　　2125

53

Now, William was the first to reach the bridge.
When he saw the Duke, he spoke to him thus:
"Duke," said the Count, "May God keep you from harm!
Must I now always guard myself from you?
We have already reached a peace accord:　　　　　2130
That peace was made at Tours, inside the church.　　　　　**2131**
We did kiss each other, before the knights."
"Truly," said Richard, "you know how to preach!
Yet you took from me my sole, eldest heir,
Who shall never sit as ruler of land.　　　　　2135

By the Apostle invoked by pilgrims,
Before you go, you shall be mistreated.
Neither God nor man shall come to your aid.
They won't keep me from cutting off your head,
And ripping all your limbs from your body." 2140
"Villain," said William, "God shall bring you harm!
I deem you no better than a mad dog!"
He pricked Alion with spurs of pure gold
And struck Richard full on his strapped long shield.
He broke through below the boss and pierced him; 2145
He gashed him and mangled his white hauberk.
With his steel blade he struck at his left flank.
Red blood flowed down from both sides of the wound.
Right quickly, the good horse tossed off its load:
And spurs were turned right up towards the sky. 2150
The point of his helmet stuck in the ground
With such great force that two laces ripped off.
Standing on him he drew his sword of steel.
I believe he sought to cut off his head,
But the fifteen knights, may God send them harm, 2155
Charged full-tilt right at William the gallant.
He who would have seen the Count fight them all,
Striking hardy blows with his sword of steel,
Would have compassion for the noble man.
His companions then came to his rescue: 2160
At once, each one struck down his opponent.
The Father of justice lent them His aid:
Without delay they struck down and killed ten;
The five others then fled covered with wounds.
Most grimly Count William pursued them all; 2165
He shamed them and called them all great villains.

54

The five survivors fled into a plain;
But William chased them, followed close behind.
In a great, loud voice he jeered and mocked them:
"Lord barons, by God the Heavenly King, 2170
How shall you endure this greatest of shame?
Your rightful lord we have vanquished and seized.

God! What courage, if you can rescue him!
They all replied: "By God, mercy, William!
Noble knight, you should be king of some land, 2175
Or emir of a strong and great country.
God have mercy! You have defeated us.
Our bowels drained on our horses.
And the strongest of us cannot now walk."
Now when William heard these words, he turned back. 2180

55

When William heard them begging for mercy,
Not one he touched, for all Montpellier's gold.
And thus quickly he pulled back his bridle.
He despoiled the ten dead men of their arms,
And then he came and trussed up Duke Richard. 2185
Like a coffer on a beast of burden,
They led him away on a fast charger.
They slowed not until they rejoined their group.
They arrived and found all their friends awake:
"Uncle William," said Bertrand the gallant, 2190
"The steel of your sword is covered in blood,
And your buckler is not fully intact:
Perchance you have begun a low affair."
William said: "Pardon me, by God, nephew!
When I left this place, riding on my horse, 2195
I saw you were weary and exhausted,
And I left you dozing and fast asleep.
But I took with me no more than two knights.
Then I met up with Duke Richard the Old,
For whom I waited the whole of the day. 2200
He had with him some fifteen hardy knights.
He reproached me for the death of his son,
And he wanted to cut off all my limbs.
But the Father of justice aided us,
So that we struck down and slaughtered ten men; 2205
Five others ran away covered with wounds.
See the arms, horses of the men we killed.
We led away Duke Richard all trussed up."
And Bertrand said: "Let us give thanks to God!"

56

"Uncle William," said Bertrand the gallant,   2210
"You've acted as though you wished not to live."
"O nephew," said William, "Do pardon me.
Glad I would have wasted my youth in pain,
If the King could not hold his great birthright."
Then they prepared to resume their journey.   2215
So much did they push themselves and hasten
That they soon reached Orleans the city.
And inside William found Louis the King,
To whom he gave up Richard his captive.
Straightaway he threw him into prison.   2220
There he stayed, or so I have heard it said,
Till he died of sorrow and feebleness.
Now, William also thought to take some rest,
Hunting in the woods and by the river;
But little rest had he all his life long.   2225
Now two envoys arrived rushing greatly:
They came right from Rome; their horses were worn;
They themselves were close to death from fatigue.
At once they sought and asked to see the King.
Right quickly they found William and Louis.   2230
They fell at his feet and cried for mercy:
"Mercy, noble Count, by God's majesty!
Kindly think a little of the maiden,
To whom you have given your pledge of faith.
Brave Guaifier of Spoleto is now dead.   2235
Then, counts, lords and peers asked for her hand,
But she will give her love only to you.
We have another matter to speak of:
Galafrez is dead, the noble Emir,
Whom you led to the font and had baptized;   2240
The Pope too has gone to his final rest.
Gui of Germany has gathered his host,
And he holds the main defenses of Rome.
All the land has been plunged into sorrow;
Noble lord, only you can now save it."   2245
At these words, William hung his head down low;
Louis also began to weep and cry.
William saw him and thought he had gone mad:

"Come now, you poor King, weak and childish!
I had thought of aiding you, guarding you 2250
Against all those who live in Christendom;
But now the whole world holds you in contempt,
And I must waste my youth in your defense,
Until you come to have all that you want. 2254
Now summon forth your vassals and barons, 2255
And the poor young squires who may come,
With their lame horses, their sorry chargers,
With their scraped, dented, and worn-out armor.
All the poor nobles who wish to serve,
And who shall come to me: I shall give them 2260
Much gold, silver, and newly struck deniers,
And Spanish horses and well-fed, good mules;
These I shall lead to the city of Rome.
In Spain I acquired so very much
That I know not what to do with it all. 2265
Never shall a freeborn man find me mean,
For I would give him all things, and much more."
And the King said: "Let God do what He will!"
Then they sealed their charters and their letters,
And sent out their envoys and men-at-arms. 2270
Now before fifteen days had come to pass,
So many men came and gathered as one,
They thought fifty thousand had assembled:
Good men-at-arms and knights in their armor.
Now of those gathered, not one went on foot, 2275
As they hurried, hastened to the rescue.
I need not tell you about all their days:
They crossed Montjeu; it was a hard passage.
They did not slow down until they reached Rome.
But they could not enter by the main gate, 2280
Because the Germans did push them all back.
Nonetheless, King Louis set up his tent,
Erected his alcubes and his brahants, 2283
Laid out his kitchen, lit all the fires.
Then Count William led away all the men, 2285
Traversing the land and laying it waste.
Then he ravaged, pillaged the whole country:
The army was rich, sated with booty.

57

Count William again led away his men.
Thereat, Gui of Germany jumped right up 2290
And spoke these words to a peer of Rome:
"O noble lord, hold your peace and listen.
Take some one thousand knights from the army,
And before these men can pitch their bright tents
Let them hear your clamor and battle cries. 2295
If you are hard-pressed, I shall come help you."
The peer replied: "Thus shall it be done."
Then most rapidly they all armed themselves,
Donning hauberks and lacing bright helmets,
Girding on swords and mounting fast chargers; 2300
From their necks they hung solid, strapped long shields;
Grasped firm in their strong hands stout hunting spears.
Then through a gate they quickly departed.
Not long afterwards a thick fog arose,
So that one could not see or even ride. 2305
Now the Franks could not guard themselves at all,
And saw not the Romans come bursting in:
They took the horses and killed the riders;
From the kitchen, they took all the rations,
And then killed the master of provisions. 2310
Then it happened that Louis fled on foot,
From tent to tent he sought to hide himself,
And cried out: "Bertrand, William, where are you?
O you sons of barons, come to my aid!
Surely God will help me; I have great need!" **2315**
Now William had gone away with his men.
Count Bertrand was the first to speak with him:
"Uncle William, we must act quickly now;
I hear a great uproar in our camp.
Surely God will help us; they have great need." 2320
And the Count replied: "Then we must ride hard
Towards Rome, with our helmets laced tight.
If we can encircle them and trap them,
And get our men to lace on helmets,
We shall win for ourselves great booty. 2325
Greater was not won since brave Guaifier's death."
They turned and galloped headlong towards Rome,

And heavy, thick fog swirled all around them.
The Romans could not guard themselves at all;
They saw nothing until William cried out: 2330
"Montjoie!" he shouted, "knights, strike hard and fast!"
And then you would have seen a hard battle:
Lance-shafts were splintered and shields were shattered,
And many hauberks were torn and shredded!
Dying men fell on those already dead! 2335
And when the men had laced on their bright helms,
They cut off the foe from front and behind.
Not a single Roman fighter escaped:
Most of them were hacked down and massacred,
And others were captured and put in chains. 2340
Thereat, the lord that led them fled away.
William followed him, fast by a hillside.
Then he shouted out to him: "Knight, return!
Or soon enough you shall die like a rogue!"
With the sharp steel of his lance he pricked him, 2345
Leaning right over the neck of his horse.
When he drew his sword to cut off his head,
Then he cried out and implored for pity:
"Gallant lord, strike not, if you are William;
Take me alive; much shall it profit you: 2350
I shall give you deniers—a hogshead full." **2351**
Then, quickly Count William came up to him,
And took from him his blade of burnished steel.
He turned the captive over to Louis,
And then he headed back to his soldiers. 2355
Thereat, Gui of Germany jumped right up,
Said to his men, "Hold your peace and listen:
Dead are all my men, hacked and massacred.
If I do not take action through battle,
And fight body to body with a knight, 2360
Then shall all our force be but for naught."

58

Gui of Germany called for an envoy,
Put him on a horse from Arabia,
On his neck he hung a great marten pelt,

Hastily thrust a baton in his hand. 2365
Gui of Germany said to his envoy:
"Hasten to the silken tents down below,
And say to Louis, son of Charles, from me
That unjustly he despoils my demesne;
He has no right over Rome, my birthright. 2370
If by great pretense he seeks to have it,
Then he must come out and fight against me,
Or send a knight in his stead to fight me. 2373
Tell him, if I am beaten in battle,
I shall quit Rome, leave it as his bequest, 2375
And none shall come strike a blow against him.
And if I conquer with my cutting sword,
He may take with him no more than a mite:
Let him go to France, to Paris, Chartres,
But Rome he shall leave as my heritage." 2380
The envoy said: "This just task I shall do."
And then he departed by the main gate.
He tarried not until he reached their camp,
And then dismounted by the silken tents.
Soon he entered the high, vast pavilion. 2385
Inside he found Louis, the son of Charles.
In front of his barons he informed him:
"Just Emperor, listen now to my words.
I shall not greet you, for it is not right.
Gui of Germany sends me as envoy. 2390
Through me you must know — I cannot hide it –
You've no right to Rome; it's not your birthright.
If by great pretense you seek to have it,
Then you must come out and fight against him,
Or send a knight in your stead to fight him. 2395
If he comes to be beaten in battle,
He shall quit Rome; leave it as your bequest;
None shall come and strike a blow against you.
And if he conquers with his cutting sword,
You may take with you no more than a mite: 2400
Return to France, to Paris, to Chartres,
But Rome you shall leave as his heritage."
The King heard all this and hung low his head.
Before he spoke, he said to his barons:
"Lord barons, listen to what I must say. 2405

Gui of Germany has insulted me.
And now he summons me to do battle;
But I am young and of a tender age,
And I cannot yet maintain my barons.
Will a brave Frank face him on my behalf?" 2410
When his barons heard him, they hung their heads.
Seeing this, the King knew not what to do;
Softly he wept into his marten furs.
And just then Count William Strongarm showed up;
He was leading his soldiers back to camp. 2415
All armed he did enter the silken tent
And saw the King sighing, sorely weeping.
When he saw this, he was filled with great rage.
Then he cried out so all the barons heard:
"O weak King, may God's body reprove you! 2420
Why do you weep? Who has come to harm you?" **2421**
And without delay Louis said to him:
"In God's name, lord, what shall I hide from you?
Gui of Germany has insulted me.
He has challenged me to single combat, 2425
And not a single Frank will now help me.
But I am young and of a tender age,
And I cannot yet maintain my barons."
"King," said William, "may God's body chide you!
Twenty-four combats have I fought for you. 2430
Do you think I shall abandon you now?
No, by God, I shall take up the challenge.
For all of your Franks are not worth one mite!"
Then to the envoy he spoke these stern words:

59

"Friend, brother," said William the gallant knight, 2435
"Go and tell Gui of Germany from me
That one knight, who seeks to defend his lord,
Will take up the challenge with great gladness.
I shall choose the hostages that I want,
And he can also choose as he wishes. 2440
The victor will take all he has promised."
Count paladin Bertrand leapt to his feet.

"Uncle," said he, "things have been bad for us.
All battles, combats have fallen to you.
Your courage has made ours as nothing. 2445
Lord, let me take on this single combat.
Allow me to engage in it for you."
The Count replied, "You speak most foolishly,
When Louis was so greatly in distress,
Not one man among you had courage, strength 2450
To dare offer his glove in his defense. 2451
Do you really think I shall now step back?
I shall not! Not for all of Abilant.
Envoy, brother, tell Gui of Germany
To arm himself and then come to the field; 2455
And facing him shall be William himself."
Then the envoy turned back and spurred away;
He did not stop until he had reached Rome.
Gui of Germany met him most promptly.
"Friend, good brother, how did you find the Franks?" 2460
"In the name of God, I shall hide nothing:
A knight, who seeks to defend his liege lord,
Shall take up the challenge, as is his wish.
He wants hostages. That is his demand.
You may take some too, if you desire: 2465
The victor shall take what has been agreed.
And William is his name, as I deem it.
Another knight leapt to his feet — Bertrand;
He is his nephew, as I understand;
He greatly sought to take up the challenge." 2470
"Friend, good brother," said Gui of Germany,
"Now, when I slay this William on the field,
I shall grant his nephew, Bertrand, his wish:
Then no more shall he go seeking combat.
Bring me my most prized and cherished weapons." 2475
And he replied: "It shall be as you wish."
They brought him his weapons without delay.
On his back they put his iron hauberk:
Red was the chain-mail like burning fire.
Then they laced on his shining green helmet; 2480
A red carbuncle gleamed on the nose-guard; 2481
On his left side he girded his broadsword,
And then they led his swift charger to him;

From the saddle-horn hung a second sword.
He leaped upon his charger right away, 2485
Using neither stirrups nor saddle-horn.
His solid targe he hung upon his neck,
And in his fist he grasped the sharpest lance,
To which five golden nails held his banner.
He left through the gate, spurring fast away, 2490
And promptly reached the meadow of Nero,
Where Count William saw him without delay.
He called out to Guiélin and Bertrand:
"My foe has come upon the battlefield;
If I linger long, then I am vanquished. 2495
Bring now to me my most cherished weapons."
They said to him: "We are at your command."
Then they brought his weapons without delay.
Louis the valorous helped to arm him.
He donned his hauberk and laced his bright helm, 2500
And on his left side he girded Joyous,
Given him by Charles, most brave in battle.
Then they led to him Alion the swift,
On which he then mounted most skillfully.
On his neck he hung a solid, strong shield, 2505
And in his strong fist grasped a good, sharp lance,
To which five golden nails held his banner.
Then he left the camp, spurring fast away,
Stopping not till he reached the battlefield.

60

Marquis William broached the high battlefield. 2510
Gui of Germany spoke these words to him:
"Who are you? Come now, do not lie to me,
You who have so much daring in your heart
That you have come to do battle with me."
"Yes," said William, "Now, I shall be forthright: 2515
I am William the son of Aimeri,
The one from Narbonne, the hardy, the brave.
I have come to fight with my blade of steel
Against you, who as I see, are inflamed.

Listen now, by what right I have come here: 2520
Rome belongs to the King of Saint Denis;
For this cause I fought in single combat,
On this field, against Corsolt the Arab,
A man of great strength, who had no mother. 2524
He it was who cut the nose on my face." 2525
When Gui heard this, he was filled with great dread;
Sought not to stay, though given rich Paris. 2527
Then he looked at William, and said these words:
"So you are indeed William the marquis,
From Narbonne, the son of Count Aimeri! 2530
Thus, let us now make peace and be good friends,
And you and I shall hold Rome together."
"O wretch," said William, "May God punish you!"
I did not come here to parlay with you.
I shall never betray my rightful lord. 2535
Never! Though I be torn from limb-to-limb."
When Gui heard this, he was filled with great dread.
He swore by the Apostle who aids Rome:
"You are vile, for nothing was asked of you.
But now I defy you, by Heaven's Lord." 2540
William replied: "And I too defy you."
Then they drew back, as far as a bowshot,
And faced each other, staring straight ahead.
The stout lances they braced upon their breasts,
And prepared to deal out hard, doughty blows. 2545
Then they pricked their horses with long, sharp spurs.
With lowered lances, they charged hard and fast.
Crushing blows they struck on their cambered shields,
And smashed the lances hard on the bosses.
But they could not gouge through the bright hauberks. 2550
Now the shafts shattered because of the shock,
And the splinters flew up, high to the sky.
Their breasts and bodies were grimly knocked back,
And sturdy, cambered shields rammed each other –
But their hauberks and horses paid the price! 2555
Helmets grated hard upon their faces,
So that blood and sweat dripped down to the ground.
Down fell the two men and the two horses.
The two horses lay full flat on the earth;
But the two fighters leapt back on their feet, 2560

With swords drawn and targes held most firmly.
Viciously they clashed, for they were not friends.

61

Now, quickly Count William leapt to his feet.
He called upon God, the Father most just:
"Saint Mary, Virgin most holy, help me! 2565
No man has ever knocked me off my horse."
Gui of Germany viciously replied:
"By God, William, prayer will not help you.
I claim Rome, its walls, and all of its fiefs.
Never shall Louis claim these as his own." 2570
"O wretch," said William, "May God destroy you!
By the Apostle invoked by pilgrims,
Before eventide, before the sun sets,
So brutally shall I thrash your body
That no one will pay one bezant for it." 2575
He grasped Joyous, with it bright blade of steel,
And he hurtled at Gui ferociously.
He struck at his metal-enforced helmet:
Costly embossing gems fell to the earth.
No more wore he a white double hauberk; 2580
Had no need for it after he was struck.
Upon his hip he did receive the blow
And more than a foot was cut from his flesh:
The bone stood out naked beneath the groin.
"See now," said William, "this blow has slain you, 2585
You have tasted the sharpness of this blade."
Gui of Germany angrily replied:
"William, may God destroy you utterly!
Do you really hope to terrify me?
This poor flesh does not last forever; 2590
But by the cross to which all pilgrims pray,
Before eventide, before the sun sets,
I shall avenge your cutting of my flesh."
He grasped his sword with its blade of bright steel,
He hurtled at William right savagely. 2595
He struck at his metal-enforced helmet:
Costly embossing gems fell to the earth;

Would no more wear the bright double hauberk,
And Count Aimeri would have had no heir.
But God did not allow this to happen. 2600
With his blow, Gui gained little advantage:
For his sword shattered at the very hilt;
But straightaway he drew out another.
Seeing this, noble William laughed in scorn.
He grasped Joyous, with its strong blade of steel, 2605
And hurtled at Gui most ferociously.
He struck his metal-enforced helmet hard,
And the blade went straight down to the shoulder,
Cutting down deep into the very breast.
By this hardy blow, he was laid low, dead. 2610
The Tiber was close by; he threw him in.
Burdened by iron, the body sank down,
So that no man could ever retrieve it. **2613**
Beholding this, William began to shout:
"Montjoie," he cried, "God, Saint Denis helped me! 2615
Thus it is that Louis has been avenged."
Then he mounted Alion his charger;
Took Clinevent—Gui's horse that he wanted.
Without delay, he rode back to the camp.
Then Bertrand his nephew came up to him, 2620
And Louis, full of joy, glad and happy.
Guielin and Gautier openly wept:
They had not known a day so full of dread,
Except when he had fought against Corsolt—
"Good uncle William, are you safe and sound?" 2625
"Yes," he answered them, "thank God in Heaven!
Good nephew Bertrand, I shall hide nothing:
I want to give you this very swift horse,
Since yesterday you wanted this combat."
Bertrand responded: "Truly, I thank you!" 2630
But the men of Rome agonized, fretted.
They said: "We have gained nothing but evil,
For gone is our master, slaughtered, killed;
Let us humble ourselves right quickly,
And let us go now and beg for mercy." 2635
They said to each other: "This we shall do."
With a great wondrous cross made of pure gold,
With reliquaries, incense, psalteries,

They carried out all the saints from the church.
Then they opened the gates without delay; 2640
They gave a good welcome to their brave lord.

62

Then did William the noble enter Rome;
He took his lord swiftly and rapidly,
And straightaway made him sit on the throne:
Thus he crowned him before the lords of France. 2645
Thereupon, he gave his most solemn oath:
This oath was sworn by all who were faithful,
And even by those who were not loyal.

63

And thus did gallant William enter Rome,
And did crown Louis his rightful liege lord: 2650
Thus did he secure all the vast domain.
Soon after he made ready to depart.
Both Louis and he traveled together,
Till they arrived in the kingdom of France.
The King went to the city of Paris 2655
And Count William to Montreuil-on-sea.
Now, William thought to take his ease at last,
Hunting in the woods and by the river;
But little rest had he all of his life,
For now the Franks rose up in great revolt, 2660
Fighting with each other most foolishly:
They burned villages and ravaged the land;
None among them sought to defend Louis. 2663
A herald came and gave William the news.
When the Count heard him, he was filled with dread. 2665
He called Bertrand: "Noble nephew, listen:
By God's love, what counsel can you give me?
The King, my lord, is disinherited."
Bertrand replied: "You must abandon him;
Cast off France — leave them all to the Devil, 2670
And even this King who is a great fool:
Soon he shall have not one foot of his fief."

And William replied: "Let us leave this talk:
In his service I have wasted my youth."
Then he summoned all his men and his friends. 2675
They all forced themselves to ride and to walk.
Thus they came to the city of Paris.
And inside William found Louis the King.
Then they began a war that was brutal.
And when Marquis William Shortnose perceived, 2680
That he could not stay on in the country,
For he had many mortal enemies,
He took the lad that he swore to protect,
And bore him to the city of Laon. 2684
Then he besieged those inside the city, 2685
And ravaged and pillaged the land without.
He dismantled the mighty defense-works,
And then broached and pulled down all the high walls.
In one year, he vanquished all the rebels,
And forced fifteen nobles to come to court, 2690
Who gave all their fiefs and inheritance
To Louis, who watched over all of France.
His sister he gave Louis in marriage. 2693
When he sat with all his barons, Louis,
Now full-grown, was most grateful to William. 2695

Notes to the Translation

12: According to medieval reckoning, the kingdoms of the world numbered ninety-nine. Perhaps a mystical number borrowed from Jewish or perhaps even Muslim traditions.

19: By A.D. 814, the Carolingian Empire included most of Western Europe. Beginning from the south, it embraced the Spanish March (most of Northern Spain along with Barcelona), Sardinia, Corsica, Sicily, the Duchy of Benevento, Naples, Lombardy, Bavaria, Pannonia, Moravia, and Bohemia. In Northern Europe, the Empire included Saxony, the Low Countries, and present day France. South of the Spanish March was the Moorish Caliphate of Cordova (Al Andalus), and to the East, beyond the Oder River were the principalities of the Slavic people. In Western Europe, only Anglo-Saxon England, the Kingdom of Denmark and Scandinavia were independent of Charlemagne's rule.

27: Aix is Aix-la-Chapelle, or present day Aachen. The "church" refers to the Capella Palatina, or Charlemagne's church, built A.D. 792–805, where he is also buried.

35: A reference to Louis VI's difficulty in dealing with the nobility of his day, who were all robber barons. It took Louis VI some twenty years to finally break the power of these barons.

41: The "Apostle of Rome" is the Pope, who is the representative of St. Peter (the first "Apostle of Rome").

42: The "offertory" is that part of the Mass that precedes canon (words of consecration), during which the alms of the congregation are collected; an anthem is usually sung as accompaniment to the offertory.

60: The fear seems to be that a foreign king will be outside the bloodline of Charlemagne and who, therefore, will lack the efficacy that Charlemagne's blood possesses. We are dealing with sacral kingship (as evidenced throughout *The Crowning*). Sacral kingship imbues magical qualities in the blood and person of the king, who then passes these qualities on to his people in the form of beneficences: fertility (for both the land and the people), peace, justice, and prosperity. In brief, the health and vigor of the king's body is mirrored in the well-being of the kingdom.

71: There is a sacred trust that kingship implies, and this trust is clearly stated by Charlemagne in the preceding lines. To betray this trust is to forfeit the crown.

75: On the River Gironde stands Bordeaux; to the south were the Moors. In A.D. 777, the Emir of Saragossa asked Charlemagne for help to fight the Emir of Cordoba. In 778, Charlemagne crossed the Pyrenees and reached the Ebro River. After successfully capturing Pamplona, he was beaten back to Saragossa. During the retreat Roland, warden of the Breton March, and some other nobles were ambushed and killed by the Basque and Navarese, in the rearguard action of Roncesvalles. In A.D. 801, the region between the Pyrenees and the Llobregat was organized as the Spanish March, with the city of Barcelona as the capital.

84: Another version of the king's trust to uphold right and vanquish wrong. A "denier" was a small silver coin, minted from the time of the Merovingians in France. The coin weighed 1–2 grams. "Denier" derives from the Latin *denarius*, a Roman coin of small value.

95: In ancient Germanic culture, the long hair of a man denoted strength and virility. This sacral quality carried over into Merovingian times, where the long hair of a king was a sign of his royalty and was invested with great magical properties. To cut the hair of a king or a prince was equivalent to maiming; and once the hair of a king or prince was cut, he could never be king again. A woman's long hair was a sign of her fertility; to cut her hair was to make her infertile. The Salic and Burgundian Codes impose heavy penalties for hair of men, women, boys and girls being forcibly cut. It was the Carolingians who destroyed the notion of associating long hair with kingship, especially in the degrading treatment of Childeric III. However, it is interesting that *The Crowning* preserves this very ancient notion of long hair, because during the time when it was composed and performed, long hair was out of fashion and considered effeminate.

97: The traditional refuge of a maimed (shorn) king was the abbey, where he spent his remaining life in the cloister. "Warden" here has the meaning of "abbot." To "pull ropes" refers to ringing church bells.

98: "Prebend" is the land from which revenue is received to support a church or abbey. Abbots from the royal line often received prebends, and were known as prebendaries.

104: It was after the age of sixteen that one became a knight.

154: This is a silver denier issued by the Counts of Anjou. An Angevin denier was worth one Tournois denier. It fell in value in the 10th century to half its value, and thus became a coin of little worth. It was used from about A.D. 987 to the end of the 13th century, when it was replaced by a Mansois denier (from Le Mans).

162: "Frank" here is the generic term for the French.

187: According to medieval bestiaries (a book of beasts wherein the nature of various animals was explained and often allegorized), a leopard was extremely bloodthirsty, and was born after a lioness had an adulterous liaison with a panther. Thus, the leopard was an animal inferior both to the lion and the panther (both considered noble beasts). Perhaps we have an affirmation of the accusation made earlier by Charlemagne that the child Louis was the son of an inferior man who had slept with the queen.

196: This advice to show great cruelty in order to subdue a nation recalls Charlemagne's campaign against the Saxons, which began in earnest in A.D. 772. The Saxons were one of the few remaining pagan peoples of Europe, and Charlemagne in effect began a holy war against them, seeking to convert them and incorporate their lands into his kingdom. The Saxon resistance was led by Widukind (A.D. 743–?807). By 775, the Saxon nobility was forced to declare itself loyal to Charlemagne; mass baptisms of the population followed. Widukind fled to Denmark. The diet at Paderborn (in 777) sealed the complete submission of the Saxons.

After the disastrous raid at Saragossa (in the summer of 778), the Saxons rose in rebellion, led by Widukind, who had returned from Denmark. The result was a long series of campaigns that lasted 32 years; it was the cruelest war fought by the Franks. In Charlemagne's eyes, the Saxons had committed treason (they had gone against the treaty signed at Paderborn), and far worse, they were guilty of apostasy, since most people who had been baptized took up their old religion right after the priests left. The punishments were severe. First, Charlemagne struck at the root of the old religion and destroyed the sacred World Tree, the holy of holies, the cosmic pillar of the Saxons, the *Irminsul*, which stood at Eresburg. Second, there were mass deportations (with the vacant land being settled by Franks). Third, all pagan shrines and sacred groves were destroyed. Fourth, anyone practicing the old pagan religion was summarily executed. And fifth, in 782, some 4500 Saxon men were beheaded in one day at Verden on the Aller. The bloody method with which the missionary task was carried out was unknown in the early Middle Ages, and Charlemagne was criticized for his relentless savagery, especially by men like Alcuin. Finally, by 804 the Saxons were fully subdued and Christianized, including Widukind (who was baptized in 785 at Attigny).

198: The Normans are shown as being unruly and prone to rejecting the authority of the French kings. By A.D. 900, Viking raiders had firmly established themselves in Northwestern France, that is, along the banks of the lower Seine and extending Northeast to the River Bresle (in Picardy) and Southwest to Saint-Malo in Brittany. The leader of the Vikings (called, in contemporary records, the "Northmen" or "Normans") was Rollo (Hrolf). He was the son an Orkney earl (Rognvald), and popularly known as *Gongu* Hrolf (Hrolf the Walker), because no horse could carry him, so fat was he. The majority of the Normans were of

Danish origin (although Rollo was probably Norwegian). Seeing that it was impossible to drive out the Norsemen, Charles the Simple (879–929), who was the grandson of Louis the Pious, gave the land upon which the Vikings had settled over to Rollo as a dukedom in A.D. 911, naming it "Normandy" or the "kingdom of the Northmen." In A.D. 912 Rollo was baptized as Robert, and promised to aid Charles against his enemies and also to keep other Viking raiders out of France. This Rollo loyally did. Rollo was succeeded by his son William Longsword; William the Conqueror was also Rollo's descendent.

207: "Provost" and "warden" are low-grade functionaries, the implication being that a person of humble origin cannot look after a job that is higher than his estate in life. Confusing the estates was a dire sin against God's order of things in the medieval mind.

230: Charlemagne was crowned the Holy Roman Emperor on Christmas Day A.D. 800 by Pope Leo III, in St. Peter's Basilica. Leo III had become pope five years earlier, but was unable to hold his position. He was attacked in 799 and his enemies sought to tear out his tongue and blind him; but he escaped to Paderborn, where he sought, and obtained, the protection of Charlemagne. He returned to Rome, this time with a large Frankish contingent and successfully maintained his position. No doubt, the crowning of Charlemagne as Emperor the following year was a gesture of thanks.

256: Literally: "God who is all spirit." A reference to the incorporeality of God the Father and God the Holy Spirit in the Trinity.

264: "Charter and seal" describes an official court document. William will come only if formally summoned by the king.

274: A sword was a knight's most prized possession, and represented his strength and power. The sword often bore a name (William's is called "Joyous") and would be handed down from one generation to the next. Thus the older the sword the better it was considered, having withstood the test of many combats. From the 10th century to the early 13th swords had a broad, double-edged blade, with a fuller down the middle, and were about 76 cm (2 feet 6 inches) long. The cross guard (quillon) would either slightly droop or sit straight. The blade could be enchased and overlaid with panels of engraved silver and gold, or bear gold filigree groundwork.

276: Helmets of the 11th and 12th century were conical, built around a framework of iron strips, and then overlaid with sheets of bronze or copper. A nasal guard was riveted to a reinforcing band around the lower rim. Most often, the nasal would be highly worked, with gold and silver inlay.

278: Lances before the 13th century were about 2m (6 feet 6 inches) long, and were made of ash wood, with a small iron or steel head. The shield in common use during the 10th–13th centuries was the "kite shield." It was long and triangular, with a rounded top, and was made of wood, iron and leather. Given the length of the shield, it protected the legs as well as the body.

289: This is William's prophetic dream of fighting the pagan horde, which has issued from Russia (the land from where pagans were thought to emerge).

292: Wolfhound is a translation of the Old French *veltre*. It is no more than a guess. In medieval bestiaries, a wolfhound was a cross between a dog and a wolf, and it was said that the female wolfhound preferred to mate with a tiger, and thus gave birth to a beast far fiercer than a lion. Perhaps *veltre* refers to this type of tiger-wolfhound; certainly the ferocity of the creature in the dream would indicate a creature more savage than an ordinary hunting dog, especially since it represents the giant Corsolt.

294: The "tree" is the church under, and for, whose protection William fights.

310: Of course, William does not fight Corsolt by the Red Sea, but by the waters of the Tiber. Perhaps this biblical allusion is meant to evoke the sense of deliverance, much as Moses delivered the Jews from Egypt and led them across the Red Sea. Further, this allusion sets the stage for the righteous believers to survive and the impious infidels to perish, as occurred in the Exodus story.

314: Here we have a direct intervention of the performer/poet, who is exploiting the "cliffhanger" part of the story in order to ask for more reward to keep on unwinding the tale.

317: The first service of the day would be Matins, which began well before dawn (around 3:00 A.M.). This was followed by Lauds at cockcrow or dawn.

318: The placing of arms on the altar is an act of dedication and sanctification. It is a very ancient tradition that goes back to pre–Christian times in Europe.

319: "Arabian gold" refers to the gold used by King Solomon to gild his Temple in Jerusalem, which came from Arabia. This gold was considered the finest and purest (hence the costliest) according to medieval tradition. Precious metals in the Middle Ages were severely debased.

325: In A.D. 846, there was a raid by the Saracens on Rome, during which they wreaked great slaughter and also desecrated many of the churches and holy places. They sacked the basilicas of Saint Peter and Saint Paul; only the strong defenses of Rome prevented them from sacking the city itself. Further threat from Saracen raiders was neutralized when their strong fleet was destroyed off the coast of Ostia by the allied fleets of Rome, Amalfi, Gaeta, and Naples—and a sea storm.

341: To touch someone on the shoulder signified a plea for help in Germanic tradition.

354: William does not want to get involved, being afraid of the might of the pagans. Cowardice is one of the sins of the warrior in Indo-European tradition.

363: William's cowardice is further heightened by his attempt at sending for help from Louis, a mere child who cannot even control his own kingdom.

370: A hauberk was a knee-length mail tunic, with front and back slit, and long in the sleeve; it weighed about 14 kg (31 lbs). Chain mail was constructed of overlapping metal scales or rings riveted to a leather or cloth garment. Each ring passed through four others for added strength and flexibility. Because the construction was labor-intensive, chain mail was very expensive. Thus for example one hauberk was valued at several oxen in the 11th century. Underneath the hauberk was a quilted tunic (an "aketon"), stuffed with straw or wool, which absorbed the force of a blow.

375: Bertrand speaks as William's conscience, seeking to shame him into action.

408: Silk came into Europe by way of Moorish Spain and was a very high-value commodity.

411: This is a secondary shield hung around the neck and used in hand-to-hand combat. The word "targe" comes from the Frankish *targa*.

413: Each knight of worth had his own standard or pennant that gave an emblematic representation of his courage and strength, a tradition found in the Germanic past.

433: To clash arms was a sign of readiness to do battle; the action consisted of striking the shield with the sword or lance.

437: An "emir" is a chieftain or prince. The word derives from the Arabic *amir* meaning "commander."

441: The treasure includes not only gold, silver and jewels, but also holy relics (of course, worthless to pagans, but formulaically included).

463: Galafrez lays his claim to the city by way of its pagan past, in contrast with the Christian claim to the city through St. Peter.

471: Ancient Carthage was renowned for its great wealth. However, it is difficult to be sure if *The Crowning* refers to the city of Dido and Hannibal, or to Cartagena in Spain.

489: Giving and taking of hostages was a common practice in ancient and medieval warfare. The fate of hostages often depended upon how the opponents fared and behaved. Also, hostages were usually highborn men and women; thus the "value" of the hostages was crucial to the exchange.

494: The story of David and Goliath is certainly at play here.

504: Corsolt is brought right close to the Pope to emphasize the Saracen's great height.

513: This humorous line also seems to reflect an anti-clerical sentiment, a theme that is persistent in *The Crowning*.

521: It was common practice to buy off an enemy. Indeed, during the later days of the Roman Empire, with increasing attacks by wandering Germanic and Hunnic tribes, Rome often paid its enemies to go away.

537: Corsolt's "pact" with God appears to represent the belief of the Cathars, a group that would later be branded as heretical and completely destroyed. The Cathars ("the pure ones") perhaps acquired their beliefs from the Bogomils of the Balkans. Essentially, they followed a dualistic faith that taught good and evil existed on equal footing in the universe, and that the world was the creation of Satan, who had led angels astray and imprisoned them in human form. Consequently, the Catholic concept of the Trinity was firmly rejected and Christ was seen, not as the Son of God, but as a holy man, a pious preacher.

Also, Corsolt recalls the heretic Tanchelm who flourished in Flanders and proclaimed himself God. He had many devotees, and his followers even went so far as to preserve the water he bathed in as a holy relic. In 1115, Tanchelm was murdered by a Catholic priest. There are shades of other heretics present in Corsolt as well; for example, Pierre de Bruys and Henry of Lausanne.

543: An overt reference to Corsolt's cannibalism.

549: The amazement stems from the fact that God has not struck down the heretic for his great blasphemy and avowed enmity.

575: An interesting anti-clerical statement that certainly suggests the clergy needs the warrior in order to sustain its priority in society.

594: Saints' relics often consisted of preserved body parts and bones.

602: The singer/poet again interjects to suggest ridicule brings harm.

621: In the Middle Ages, Mohammad and Cahut were often mentioned together as a pair of pagan gods.

637: Cuirass was plating for the breast and the back. This was an archaic form of armor and was replaced by the hauberk before the 9th century. It is interesting that Corsolt wears both a cuirass and a double-mail hauberk, perhaps to emphasize his invulnerability.

661: A seneschal was the steward of a nobleman; he looked after all domestic affairs of the manor. The word is Germanic in origin and means "old servant" (*sene*: "old"; *scalh*: "servant").

667: A mace was very effective against chain mail since it bludgeoned the opponent. A mace consisted of a wooden truncheon with metal spikes towards the top. This was the weapon often used by fighting clergymen (the clergy was forbidden to shed blood, but they could break bones). For example, in the Bayeux Tapestry, Bishop Odo (William the Conqueror's half-brother) is shown fighting with such a spiked mace.

669: Corsolt's cannibalism is now made manifest.

675: Authorial interjection to explain the embarrassing cowardice shown by William earlier in the *laisse*.

679: William's prayer is to preserve the horse.

689: William's efficacious prayer summarizes the main events in Jesus' life. The prayer juxtaposes William's fight with the evil Corsolt and Jesus' own struggle with the Devil and the pagans of his day.

693: The medieval mind was greatly imbued with fear of the Devil and daily life was much concerned with deflecting his assaults and lures.

701: By the Middle Ages the tradition that Adam and Eve ate an apple (the forbidden fruit) was well established. Although the Old Testament mentions only a "fruit" forbidden to the first human pair, later tradition associated that "fruit" with the apple — perhaps drawing upon the non–Christian association of the apple with sexuality. This connection appears as early as the 3rd century in the writings of Clement of Alexandria (who died ca. A.D. 215).

726: This is an obscure reference to an equally obscure saint. Legend has it that Anastasia was present at the birth of Jesus. She wanted to hold the child but could not since she had no hands. Miraculously, she grew hands and was able to hold the infant Jesus. There are two Anastasias. The first is known as St. Anastasia the Widow, who was martyred during the reign of the Emperor Diocletian in A.D. 304. She is commemorated every Christmas Day by the saying of the second Mass in Rome by the Pope. The second saint is known as Anastasia the Elder who was martyred during the reign of Valerian in A.D. 249.

729: The tradition of the three kings is specifically medieval since the New Testament does not mention that the wise men who came from the East to pay homage to Jesus were kings or were even three in number (Matthew 2). However, by the 7th century A.D., it was believed that the "wise men" were three kings (their number probably derived from the number of gifts they presented to the baby Jesus).

735: The story of the murder of the Innocents is given in Matthew 2:16–18. It relates King Herod's attempt to kill the infant Jesus. The number is specifically medieval in origin, since the New Testament does not give a specific number.

744: The "Golden Gates" are the *Portae Aureae* (one of the gates of Jerusalem), through which, medieval tradition asserted, Jesus entered on Palm Sunday. The Gospels do not mention the name of the gate.

756: Methuselah was an Old Testament patriarch who is said to have lived for 969 years. See Genesis 5:27.

757: Jews were held responsible for the death of Jesus in the Middle Ages, and consequently there was a deep-seated hatred of them — a condition no doubt aggravated by the fact that many members of the nobility were indebted to Jews (who practiced money-lending, one of the few trades open to them). This blame upon the Jews stemmed from the Gospel accounts (Matthew 27:15–25; Mark 15:6–14; Luke 23:13–25; 18:38–40). Jewish persecution, in France, is first evident in Burgundy under King Sigismund (A.D. 517). Violence is first evidenced during the time of the First Crusade (1096–1099), when the crusaders slaughtered Jews in many cities and towns. And again in the Second Crusade (1147–1149) there were fresh atrocities. In 1171, the Jews of Blois were burned on the charge that they were using Christian blood in the Passover. This allowed Philip Augustus, in 1180 (the year of his accession), to confiscate all the unmovable goods of his Jewish subjects and to banish them from his domain.

768: Longinus or Longeus was the blind Roman soldier who pierced the side of Jesus with his spear; he applied the gushing blood to his eyes and recovered his sight. The New Testament (John 19:34) does not mention the name of the soldier nor that he was blind. Certainly, no Roman army legion would have blind soldiers in active duty. However, it is interesting to note that the ancient god Baldur (who was the resurrecting god in Germanic myth) was killed by the blind god Höder, with a spear made from the mistletoe. Most likely, Germanic myth has melded into Christian belief.

782: The journey of Christ into Hell to rescue the righteous pagans mirrors William's impending struggle to rescue Rome and Christianity from the pagan (Devilish) threat.

810: Corsolt's offer is exactly the same as the Pope's, only it lacks the promise of salvation.

828: Aimers shuns human habitation in imitation of hermits who perpetually sought desolate spots to live in. As a warrior-hermit, his vow is to strike down Saracens, or the enemies of God.

834: Hearing that Aimers has killed many Saracens, Corsolt now seeks revenge for the murder of his kinsmen. The battle between the two has moved from the realm of the political to a personal vendetta.

840: Another presentation of the heretical view that the Devil created and ruled the earth.

844: Corsolt derides the sacraments (sacred rituals) of the church. His remark about Christianity's folly echoes the comment found in I Corinthians 1:18 that Christianity is foolishness to those who perish (the unsaved). Since Corsolt is a pagan and about to perish, he finds Christian belief to be foolish. Therefore, to the medieval mind, Corsolt has already condemned himself.

853: Corsolt's derision of Christianity is answered by William with this story of Mohammad, the founder of Islam. This demonization of Mohammad has its roots in the 9th century when Europe was actively fighting to contain the Arab threat that had overcome Visigothic Spain.

866: Threatening contradicts the warrior code of heroic combat, since it seeks to frighten the opponent with words rather than to overcome him with physical prowess.

888: Charlemagne as the Holy Roman Emperor was the sovereign of Rome and the Pope had his office by virtue of the Emperor's authority.

908: William realizes that he is being closely watched by the defenders of Rome. Therefore, his combat with Corsolt is not merely a personal attempt to destroy the Saracens, but is also a grand spectacle.

945: According to Germanic tradition, old weapons and armor were deemed solid and durable (and hence greatly valued), since they had survived the test of many battles. Weapons and armor were always handed down from one generation to the next.

957: This is a very brief prayer for protection, where William specifically mentions St. Loth. This is Lot of Genesis 19, the Old Testament patriarch and the nephew of Abraham, who escaped the destruction of Sodom and whose wife turned into a pillar of salt. It is important to note why William mentions Lot—for William too seeks to escape destruction.

971: Corsolt's sword is stuck in the earth and his old cuirass has not stopped William's blow.

975: This is a shorter version of the earlier prayer (ll. 695–789).

977: Recent studies have shown the earth was visualized as being round in the Middle Ages. The assumption that the medieval mind deemed the earth to be flat, and that one would fall off the edge, does not have bearing in the medieval scientific literature. This "medievalness" is a 19th century trope for the ignorance of the past. For example, Isidore of Seville (A.D. 560–636) in his *Etymologies*, Book 14 speaks of the rotundity of the earth, comparing it to a wheel. Some centuries on, William of Conches (born ca. 1100) also states that the earth is round in his *Dialogue on Natural Philosophy*. However, it is difficult to know what these thinkers meant by the earth's "rotundity." If the earth were like a wheel as Isidore stated, then *The Crowning*'s notion of the earth resting on a plinth (as on an axle) would make sense.

986: Baratron is the name for the pit of Hell, and derives from the Greek *barathron* ("pit," "gulf"). In Athens, the word signified a cleft into which criminals were thrown.

987: Beelzebub is the name of Satan. The name is a mixture of Aramaic and Hebrew and perhaps means either "Lord of the flies," or "Lord of the High House." Satan would certainly be the master of Hell (his own "High House"). References to Beelzebub occur both in the Old and New Testaments: II Kings 1:2, Matthew 12:24–29, and Luke 11:15–22. Nero (A.D. 37–68) was the last Emperor of the Julio-Claudian line and reigned A.D. 54–68. In history he is known for his great excesses and his severe persecution of the Christians. It is held that during these persecutions, in A.D. 67, Saints Peter and Paul were killed in Rome.

1012: This description of Redemption Day also illustrates the realm of the good king as defined by Charlemagne earlier (ll. 62–67; 80–84; 174–186).

1013: The Confession is the Roman Catholic sacrament of penance, or the forgiveness of sins.

1014: According to tradition, St. Peter was crucified upside down, since he did not wish to be crucified like Jesus. This tradition does not come from the New Testament but from two early Christian writers, namely, Tertullian (born ca. A.D. 160) and Origen (A.D. 185–232). "Nero's field" refers to the gardens (and the "circus") of Nero where Peter is thought to have been crucified, along with many other Christians. The Neronian persecution of the Christians began in A.D. 64 and ended with Nero's death in A.D. 68. Tacitus (ca. A.D. 56–?115) in his *Annals* (15.44.3-7) describes gruesome scenes of torture and death that took place in Nero's gardens.

1015: The conversion of St. Paul on the road to Damascus is described in the New Testament (Acts 9:1–21). Tradition maintains that Paul was killed on the same day as Peter, during the Neronian persecution, at a place called Acquae Silviae (now Tre Fontane), near Rome.

1016: Jonah was an Old Testament prophet, and his story of surviving in the belly of a giant sea creature is mentioned in the Old Testament in the book of Jonah 1&2. The story is also mentioned in the New Testament (Matthew 12:40–41 and 16:4; Luke 11:29–32). The idea that the sea creature was a "whale" is a medieval tradition.

1017: Saint Simeon Stylites the Elder was born in present-day Northern Syria in A.D. 388, and after his death in A.D. 459 was buried in Antioch. Simeon is known as the "pillar (stylites) hermit" because he chose to stand or sit on a pillar (some 50 feet in height) in order to mortify the flesh and do penance. Legend has it that he stayed on his pillar for 36 years. His fame spread throughout the Christian world and Byzantine Emperors such as Theodosius and Leo greatly venerated him.

1018: The story of Daniel in the den of lions is related in the Old Testament (Daniel 6). It was also Daniel who interpreted the writing on the wall for King Balshazzar (Daniel 5).

1019: The story of Simon Magus ("Simon the magician") is told in the New Testament (Acts 8:9–24). Simon proclaimed himself as "the great power of God" and his teaching was likely a blend of Gnosticism and Hebrew messianic beliefs. In Christian tradition, he is called "the father of heresies," being the first one to offer an alternative to Christianity. The New Testament does not describe the fate of Simon; church literature does, such as the *Pseudo-Clementines* and the apocryphal *Acts of Saint Peter*. From the context of "being struck down," it is probable William is referring to the apocryphal *Acts of Saint Peter* where Simon is literally struck down (and dies of his injuries). In the Roman Forum, before Nero (whom he sought to convert to his beliefs), he rose up into the air to demonstrate his power. But Peter and Paul also invoked the power of their faith through prayer, and as a result Simon fell from the great height he had risen to, and died of his injuries.

1021: The episode of the burning bush is mentioned in Exodus 3:2.

1035: Aragon was much prized for its horses in the Middle Ages.

1042: The humor of William's shortened nose lies in the implied sexual innuendo.

1049: Joyous is the name of William's sword; it is also the name of Charlemagne's sword according to tradition. Later on, we are told that Charlemagne gave Joyous to William (l. 2502).

1065: The Pope is "shaming" the saint into action, just as Bertrand had shamed William into action.

1074: The picture of Corsolt as a "raving beast" recalls William's dream earlier.

1103: Corsolt assumes he has defeated William and taunts him with the idea that Louis will have to ransom him and thus William will be forever in the monarch's debt.

1117: A chain mail cowl was often worn beneath the helmet for added protection.

1149: Montpellier (in the modern *department* of Hérault) was an important market of precious metals, especially gold, in the Middle Ages.

1180: "The Apostle" is Saint Peter.

1211: It is difficult to know precisely around which two hills the pagans are being chased, since Rome is surrounded by various hills. Encircling the city are the famous "seven hills," namely, the Quirinal, the Viminal, the Esquiline, the Capitoline, the Caelian, the Palatine, and the Aventine. The city of Rome sits on a plain and is hemmed in by the Alban hills to the south, the Palestrina, Tivoli and Sabine hills to the east, and the Umbrian hills and Monte Tolfa to the north.

1315: It is interesting to note that William associates bread eating with Christianity and civilization; we noted earlier that Corsolt stood outside the pale of Christian society as a cannibal. Claude Lévi-Strauss's structure of the raw and the cooked is at play here.

1318: The greyhound was a dog exclusive to the aristocracy in the Middle Ages and, as such, it represented virtues of the Christian warrior, such as faith and strength. Thus for Galafrez to be daubed with the blood of a greyhound implies his symbolic association with Christian knighthood.

1369: The landless knight is literally a free-lance, a mercenary, and thus remains outside aristocratic society, since nobility meant ownership of land. Guaifier's daughter will bring William land as part of her dowry.

1372: A palmer was a pilgrim who had returned from Jerusalem (which the Crusaders captured in 1099). The medieval pilgrim carried two palm leaves in saltire to show that he had been to the Holy Land; hence the term "palmer."

1377: Another authorial interjection, which again indicates the time of performance (perhaps morning to afternoon).

1416: This poignant statement is borne out by other *chansons de geste* in the William cycle, where we learn that William did not marry Guaifier's daughter, but instead married Orable.

1433: There seems to be a lapse in chronology here, since at this point William has not met Orable. However, this authorial interjection does point to the fact that William did marry Orable and the audience would have known that. The author has to justify in some way the introduction of a prospective bride for William. Orable was a Saracen queen who was married to Tibalt of Africa and was the daughter of King Desramed. She lived in Orange and helped William capture the city. Thereafter, she was baptized, took the name of Guibourg, and married William — who now had a wife and a fief. The story is told in the epic *Prise d'Orange*, which dates from the 12th century.

1454: The garb of a pilgrim was like a uniform that could be immediately recognized. A typical medieval pilgrim (invariably male) wore a coarse woolen tunic; a woolen sash draped his neck. His head was protected by a wide-brimmed hat; around his waist was tied a pouch for money; and he carried a stout staff.

1458: The reference is to the cathedral of Tours, which housed the relics of Saint Martin. The cathedral was a famous place of pilgrimage in the Middle Ages, but in 1562 it was destroyed, along with the saint's relics, by militant Protestants. Small fragments of Saint Martin's tomb were found during construction excavation in 1860. Saint Martin was born in Pannonia (in modern-day Hungary) in A.D. 316 and eventually became the bishop of Tours where he died of natural causes in A.D. 397; he was the first non-martyred saint.

1477: Here we find an interesting parallel between Christ's betrayal and that of Louis.

1514: The meaning is the prospective king will not lose his senses because of pride.

1596: In medieval bestiaries, the boar is noted for its savagery and unpredictable wildness.

1603: Medieval symbolic gestures are little studied and little understood. Indeed, it is difficult to know how the movements of the body were "read" by people in the Middle Ages. William's holding of a glove in his right hand certainly suggests defiance.

1649: Physical appearance was an important concept in the Middle Ages (but is as yet little studied), since the body was the embodiment of the Word, and was described as the "temple of God." Thus, well-proportioned physical beauty reflected innate nobility. Consequently, in medieval art, we see the human body stylized to represent a type, a class. In other words, a king looked a certain way, as did a peasant; the one could never look like the other.

1663: Killing a priest or a person who could read and write was prohibited in the Middle Ages (a legality that existed in England until the 16th century. It was by virtue of this "technicality" that the English playwright Ben Jonson escaped the hangman's noose).

1757: The medieval world sought stability and order; anything that upset stability was seen as either vanity or diabolical. Therefore, society moved in prescribed social ranks, which could never merge. At the top was the king, then his nobles and knights, the clergy, and last the commoners. Each rank was obligated to the one above it. This social order was divinely ordained, and to go against it meant going against God.

1767: The number of kisses is no doubt significant, but we cannot know in which sense — perhaps as symbolic of protection or allegiance.

1776: This gnomic couplet again emphasizes the need for loyalty to one's lord — a theme that permeates the entire epic literature of this period.

1789: The herald's staff has a long pedigree, going back to Homer and to the Roman *caduceus* (a staff about 18 inches long with a white ribbon tied at the top). Such a staff marked the herald and ensured his safety in the enemy camp; harming or slaying a herald was an unthinkable, heinous offense.

1791: Lying is another of William's sins; however he lies for tactical reasons to see if Acelin really honors Louis and William and will join them despite the "fact" they only have forty men. This is a test of Acelin's character.

1795: A version of the formulaic phrase "Montpellier's gold." The reference to Avalon is either to the city of Avallon (present-day Yonne) in Burgundy, or more probably to Arthur's mythical resting place. The legend of Arthur was widespread by 1140.

1817: Acelin is subverting the divine order of society by questioning the right of Louis to be king. Since kingship was still emerging from its Germanic tradition where a king was elected from a group of nobles, the rule of primogeniture and hereditary kingship is a very central theme in *The Crowning*—just as Abbot Suger defended the right of Louis VI to crown his son king.

1823: Mangon or mancus was a Carolingian gold coin used from A.D. 400 to about A.D. 1000. Perhaps it was equal to the double-bezant, but it is difficult to know. Since gold was seriously debased in the Middle Ages, stress is placed on "fine" or "pure" gold.

1891: This is reminiscent of *The Song of Roland*; however, unlike Roland, William does not hesitate to call for help. A horn was an integral part of a Germanic warrior's battle gear.

1910: The implication is that William will force the crown on the head of the pretender and knock his brains out.

1934: William wants to kill Acelin in an ignoble way, therefore he strikes him not with the weapon of a noble warrior (a sword), but with a peasant's agricultural tool.

1967: William mutilates Richard so he can never be king, and for added measure he also cuts off his hair, which was another method of disfiguring someone of royal blood.

1976: The "kiss of peace" between Richard and William is curious since Richard has had his hands and feet hacked off. When Richard again appears in *Laisse* 50 and 52, this fact is completely ignored. It is difficult to know if the two have sworn a Peace of God or a Truce of God; the former is permanent and the later is temporary. Under both these types the two opponents were forbidden to fight by the church at designated times and holy days, nor were they permitted to destroy church property, nor harm consecrated persons, such as the clergy and the poor. If William and Richard have sworn a Truce of God (a temporary cessation of hostilities), then William's later action of hostility towards Richard makes sense.

1993: In the service of the crown William is ready to slay even a priest—an odious sin in the eyes of the church.

2036: Julian is the lord of the city of St. Giles.

2095: Broadswords of the 12th century were highly decorated, and often housed a saint's relic in the pommel, a practice carried over from pagan Germanic tradition.

2125: Since William is planning to break the peace accord, he needs the approval of his peers, as well as their witness that Richard is the aggressor.

2131: William is reminding Richard of the importance of their accord. However, William is the aggressor and breaks either the Truce of God or the Peace of God, a formal peace accord vouchsafed by the church.

2254: William's reproach is a statement of resentment in that he is wasting his years upholding Louis' rule—rather than winning land and wealth for himself.

2265: This is authorial anticipation, since in the time frame of *The Crowning*, William has not gone to Spain. That journey is recounted in another epic: *Le Charroi de Nîmes*.

2283: "Alcubes" and "brahants" are types of elaborate tents. The derivation of alcube is undoubtedly Arabic and may refer to the region south of Valencia, more specifically around Alicante and Castellar (important centers of the cloth trade). The word "alcube" means "protection." Brahant refers to the Duchy by that name (in modern-day Netherlands); it was renowned for the quality of its woven goods. The implication is that Louis has rare and costly tents.

2315: The cowardly (and childish) nature of Louis is highlighted as he runs from tent to tent weeping and seeking aid.

2351: The Old French *mui* literally means a barrel in which wine is stored (cf. modern French *muid*). One Parisian *mui* in the Middle Ages equaled 274 liters or about 75 gallons.

2365: The marten pelt and the baton are symbols of the herald.

2373: Gui's demands are similar to the ones made by Corsolt and Galafrez.

2421: William's reproach, as previously, underscores Louis' cowardice and weakness.

2451: The offer of the glove equals a warrior's commitment to protect and fight for his rightful lord—a solemn oath always sworn in the church and upon holy relics.

2481: According to medieval lapidaries, the carbuncle (or the ruby) was a most efficacious stone which lent those who possessed it ardor of heart, protection from evil, and invulnerability from wounds—thus it was especially favored by warriors (a tradition brought to the West by the Arabs who adopted it from India). It was also said the carbuncle shone in the dark with its own fire, since carbuncles served as eyes for dragons; and large snakes used the heat from the glowing stones to incubate their eggs. Because of its blood-red color, the carbuncle also represented the sacrifice of Jesus on the cross.

2524: According to ancient and medieval traditions, giants were chthonic, in that they "grew" from the earth and did not undergo human birth.

2527: Since William has no fief of his own, the gift of Paris, the seat of kings, would be the highest beneficence he could imagine.

2575: A bezant was a Roman gold coin introduced by the Emperor Constantine (A.D. ?274 or ?288–337); it weighed 65 to 70 troy grains. The bezant was the basis of trade in the Western world from A.D. 4th to the 12th centuries.

2613: By throwing Gui's body into the Tiber, William is refusing him Christian burial—thus assuring him of a fate in Hell, according to the medieval mind.

2645: William crowns Louis (a process long delayed) in front of the barons, since traditionally the king was elected at a gathering of all the nobility.

2663: The barons do not rise up to defend Louis, despite the fact they were present at his crowning—which implies that they accepted his kingship as legitimate. This is seen as betrayal.

2684: Laon is the ancient cathedral city northwest of Soissons; it was the stronghold of Carolingian kings in the 10th century.

2693: Louis marries Blanchefleur, the sister of William.

Glossary

Abel: Second son of Adam and Eve, who is killed by his brother Cain. See Genesis 4.

Acelin: The son of Duke Richard of Normandy; killed in a disgraceful manner by William.

Adam: The first man created by God in the Garden of Eden. See Genesis 2.

Aimeri: Count of Narbonne, husband of Hermeniart, and the father of seven sons: Bernard de Brabant, Bovon de Comarchis, William of Orange, Hernant li Roux, Garin d'Anseune, Aimers le Chaitif, and Guibert d'Andrenas. Narbonne was an important city in the early Middle Ages, serving as a port and as a center for the cloth trade in the Languedoc region. In A.D. 719 it was captured by the Moors, until Pepin the Short drove them out (A.D. 759).

Aimers: Younger brother of William of Orange, known in epic tradition as the "puny" (*le chaitif, le chétis*).

Aix: Aix-la-Chapelle, now Aachen (in the North Rhine-Westphalia region of Germany), was the capital of Charlemagne's empire, and where he also resided. He is buried in the Capella Palatina (modern-day Aachener Dom), a cathedral he built in A.D. 792–805.

Aliaume: Also Alelme. An obscure nephew of William who delivers a message to Acelin; he is not found elsewhere in French epic literature.

Alibant: Probably ancient Abila (modern-day Nebi-Abil) in the Lebanon.

Alion: The wondrous horse belonging to Corsolt, taken by William as a prize.

Alori: An ancestor of Richard of Rouen.

Amarmonde: A king from Bordeaux.

Anastasia (Saint): There are two saints with the same name: St. Anastasia the Widow, who was martyred during the reign of the Emperor Diocletian in A.D. 304; and St. Anastasia the Elder who was martyred during the reign of Valerian in A.D. 249.

Andernas: An unidentifiable Saracen city in Spain.

Angelier: Also Engelier. One of the Twelve Peers of Charlemagne's army. In the *Song of Roland*, he is said to be from Gascon.

Anjou: Region around the Loire River. The Franks took possession of Anjou in the 5th century, and eventually (in the 9th century) it became a county under Charlemagne. By the 10th century it was ruled by the first line of the counts of Anjou. It was an important agricultural area.

Annadore: Modern-day Andorra in the Pyrenees. The link with Charlemagne can be traced back to the legend that the Emperor stayed at one of the parishes (El Puy d'Olivesa) during his campaign against the Moors. It is also said Charlemagne gave Louis the Pious a charter, which established Andorra's independence. The six original parishes of Andorra are first mentioned in the church records of the Cathedral of Seu d'Urgell in A.D. 839.

Arabia: The homeland of the Saracens.

Aragon: The Christian kingdom of Northern Spain. It was part of the Carolingian empire until the 9th century, after which time it was ruled independently as a sovereign country under Ramiro (died 1063) and Alfonso the Warrior, who captured Saragossa from the Moors in 1118.

Archbishop: Turpin, Archbishop of Rheims, who is a prominent figure in *The Song of Roland*, and one of the Twelve Peers.

Arneïs d'Orléans: A traitor who would be king; killed by William. He is not found in any other legend associated with Charlemagne, nor is he attested in history. However, one of Charlemagne's counselors opposed the rule of Louis; his name was Wala, and he was banished to a monastery. One of Wala's associates was a count of Orléans named Mathfrid who, during the reign of Louis the Pious, was accused of treason (in that he sided with Louis' rebellious sons) and publicly humiliated in A.D. 828; Agobard of Lyons addresses a letter to him. Perhaps Arneïs is modeled on this count from Orléans.

Ascension: The day Christ rose to heaven (40 days after Easter).

Avalon: Perhaps the mythical resting place of Arthur; or perhaps Avallon (modern-day Yonne) in Burgundy.

Baratron: From the Greek *barathron* ("cleft," "pit"). The pit of Hell.

Bavaria: An ancient duchy in Southern Germany. The area was Christianized by Saint Boniface. In A.D. 788, Charlemagne defeated the Bavarian ruler Duke Tassilo III and annexed Bavaria to his empire. Thereafter, Bavaria was ruled by the Carolingians—until 911, when the area again fell into the hands of the dukes of Bavaria, who continuously rebelled against imperial authority. Bavaria was a rich agricultural area and had strategic military importance.

Beelzebub: A common medieval term for the Devil; also a Saracen god since Saracens were said to worship devils.

GLOSSARY

Béranger: One of the Twelve Peers, companion of Haton. In *The Song of Roland*, he is killed by the Saracen Grandoyne.

Bernard: William's oldest brother and father of Bertrand and Guiélin.

Berry: A duchy of medieval France whose capital was Bourges.

Bertrand: The Paladin and William's nephew and his most constant companion. He is the son of Bernard of Brabant.

Bethlehem: The city in the West Bank where Jesus was born. The Emperor Constantine built the Church of the Nativity here in A.D. 333, which was then enlarged by Justinian I in the 6th century. It is said Saint Jerome (?386–?420) translated the Bible into the Vulgate (common Latin) in the court of this church. Jerusalem was held by the Crusaders from 1099 to 1187.

Blanchefleur: The daughter of Aimeri of Narbonne and sister of William; she marries King Louis.

Bordeaux: Capital of the medieval duchy of Aquitaine.

Bovon: Also, Buevon or Beuves de Comarchis. One of William's older brothers. A *chanson de geste*, entitled *Beuves de Comarchis*, describes his adventures.

Brabant: A province in modern-day Belgium. Brabant was a *pagus* (province) in the Carolingian empire, extending from the River Schelde to the River Dijle. From the 10th to the 12th centuries, Brabant was held by the counts of Louvain who enlarged the territory considerably, so that by the 12th century Brabant included Uccle-Brussels, the abbeys of Gembloers and Nijvel, the domains of Antwerp and Orthen and as far north as 's-Hertogenbosch (Bois-le-Duc). Throughout the Middle Ages, Brabant was an important place for recruiting mercenaries.

Brie: The southeast part of Ile-de-France, between Paris and the boundary of Champagne.

Brittany: A dukedom during Carolingian times, given to Nominoë by Louis the Pious in A.D. 824. Nominoë remained loyal to Louis, but when Charles the Bald took the throne Nominoë declared Brittany independent, and the dukedom remained so until 1532 when François I signed the "Traité d'Union Perpétuelle."

Cahut: A Saracen god, often paired with Mohammed, in Old French epic.

Cain: The eldest son of Adam and Eve who killed his brother Abel. See Genesis 4.

Calabria: The region of Southern Italy that forms the "toe" of the Italian "boot." It was the Roman Bruttium, but was renamed Calabria in the 8th century under Frankish rule and added to Charlemagne's empire. Calabria was taken by the Normans under Robert Guiscard (1015–1085) and became part of the Norman kingdom of Sicily. After 1282, it became part of Naples.

Calvary: Or Golgotha ("the place of the skull"). The hill outside Jerusalem where Jesus was crucified. See Matthew 27:33; Mark 15:22; Luke 23:33; John 19:17.

Capua: The Italian city north of Naples, and the seat of King Guaifier. Capua was part of the Lombard kingdom and when Charlemagne invaded Northern Italy in A.D. 787, control of Capua went to its *gastald* (or count) Landulf I (815–843). By the end of the 9th century, Capua was a third state in the old Beneventan principality.

Carthage: A generic fief of the Saracens in Old French epics. The Roman city (Carthago-Novo: "New Carthage"), present-day Cartagena, fell to Swinthila, king of the Visigoths, in A.D. 623. Cartagena remained in Visigothic hands until A.D. 711 when the Berber chief Tarik defeated the last Visigothic king (Roderic, who ruled for just one year) and made Cartagena part of Murcia. Tarik gave his name to "Jabal Tarik" ("the mountain of Tarik"), what we now call Gibraltar.

Champion: A Saracen and nephew of King Galafrez.

Charlemagne: A.D. 742–814. Son of Pepin the Short (A.D. 714–768) and Bertrada. After his father's death, he became the king of the Franks, and eventually the Holy Roman Emperor, defender of Rome and Christendom. He was the father of Louis the Pious.

Chartres: The city of Chartres is situated on the Eure River, east of Paris, in the Beauce region. Chartres was an important pilgrimage center where the veil of Mary (Sancta Camisia) was housed. The veil was given by Charles the Bald (Charlemagne's grandson) in A.D. 858, after the church was destroyed by Viking raiders. In A.D. 911, legend has it that Rollo besieged Chartres, but he was shown the veil from the walls of the city, causing the Viking raiders to flee. Chartres also had a cathedral university, where the renowned scholar Fulbert taught ca. A.D. 980. Intellectual life flourished in Chartres until the 13th century, when it was eclipsed by Paris.

Ciquaire: A Roman with whom William lodges.

Clinevent: The war-horse of Gui of Germany.

Comarchis: Probably Commercy on the Meuse, south of Verdun.

Corsolt: A Saracen king and a hideous giant; he is the nephew of King Galafrez. He cuts William's nose but is eventually killed by him in single combat.

Cotentin: The peninsula of Normandy between Cherbourg and Avranches. This area was heavily raided by the Vikings in the 9th century. The raiders were largely Anglo-Dane and Hiberno-Norse Vikings who set up permanent camps by A.D. 851, from where they made incursions into Paris. By 867, the Northmen had become permanent settlers in the area that would become Normandy (the Frankish district of Neustria).

Cremuz: A Saracen king; his name means "frightening."

Cross: The cross on which Jesus was crucified. Tradition states that it was discovered by Saint Helena in A.D. 320 in Jerusalem. A cult of the cross had developed in the city as early as A.D. 628.

Dagobert: A Saceren king from Peralada; not to be confused with the Merovingian king of the Franks.

Daniel: An Old Testament prophet who served King Nebuchadnezzar in Babylon. The story of his interpretation of the "writing on the wall" during the feast of Belshazzar, and his survival in the den of lions (during the reign of King Darius), highlight his life. See the book of Daniel 5 and 6.

Dénis (Saint): Also Dionysius. He is the patron saint of France. The first bishop of Paris who was martyred in A.D. 270 and buried beside the Seine River, where a small chapel was soon built. By the 6th century, the chapel had become an important center of pilgrimage. In A.D. 630, King Dagobert founded a Benedictine abbey and replaced the original chapel with a large basilica. In A.D. 750, Charlemagne replaced the basilica with a new church. The present Gothic church is the work of Abbot Suger and was commenced in 1140. The Church of Saint Dénis has long been the burial place of French kings, starting with Dagobert. The banner of the Abbey, the "Oriflamme" ("gold-flame") became the standard of the French kings.

Ernaut: Also Ernald of Gironde, a brother of William. Gironde could be in Aquitaine, but more likely refers to Gerona in Catalonia, Spain.

Estolt de Langres: One of the Twelve Peers, but not mentioned in *The Song Roland*.

Eve: The first woman and wife of Adam, who listened to the serpent and ate the forbidden fruit, which caused the first human couple to be thrown out of paradise. See Genesis 2.

France: There are three descriptions of "France" in *The Crowning*. First, the Frankish kingdom of Charlemagne extending from the Elbe to the Ebro. Second, the Kingdom of France constituted in A.D. 843 (*Francia Occidentalis*). And third, the Duchy of France or of Paris, appanage of the Capetian kings, namely, Ile-de-France and the Orléanais.

Frank: The Germanic tribe that ruled Gaul from the end of the 5th century; their empire reached its greatest size under Charlemagne.

Gabriel (Saint): The Archangel who announced to Mary that she would give birth to Jesus. See Luke 1:26.

Galafrez: High king of all the Saracens and commander of the forces that have invaded Capua and Rome in *The Crowning*.

Garin: Also Guarin of Anseüne; brother of William. Anseüne is probably the pre–Roman *oppidum* of Ensérune, southwest of Béziers, in Hérault.

Gautier: Also Gaultier (or Walter). Several men bear this name: Gautier of Toulouse or Tudèle, one of William's nephews, Gautier the Abbot of St. Martin of Tours, Gautier de l'Hum (also called Ogier the Dane), one of the Twelve Peers, and Gautier the priest at St. Martin's.

Gérin: One of the Twelve Peers.

Germany: The province of Allemannia (Alemaigne), or the area inhabited by the Alemanni (literally, "various peoples") a conglomerate of various Germanic tribes. Allemannia was part of Charlemagne's empire, and extended from Mainz to Lake Constance (including Alsace).

Gironde: The river in Aquitaine where Bordeaux is located, or Gerona in Catalonia, Spain.

Golden Gates: One of the gates of Jerusalem. The *Portae Aureae* ("golden gates") through which Jesus came into Jerusalem on Palm Sunday. The name of the gates is not mentioned in the Gospels.

Guaifier: King of Capua; originally from Spoleto. In history, we find a prince of Salerno, named Guaifier, who fought against the Saracens and survived a long siege from A.D. 871-873; he was saved by Louis II, the son of Lothair. He finally freed himself from the Saracen threat by a treaty, a move much opposed by the Vatican. He fell ill soon after and saw in this the hand of God, since he had forged friendship with His enemies. He eventually became a monk and died in A.D. 879.

Gualdin: Known as "the Brown." A marquis and nephew of William.

Gui of Germany: Pretender to the imperial throne in Rome. Killed by William in single combat. There was a Gui, duke of Spoleto, who briefly ruled the disintegrating empire of Charlemagne (after the Emperor's death). In A.D. 888, Gui and Béranger, Duke of Friuli, divided the empire between themselves, with France under Gui and Italy under Béranger. However, Gui did not last long in France and was soon ousted. Thereupon, he returned to Italy and wrested power from Béranger's hands. Béranger appealed to Otto of Germany who came to his aid. Instead of a pitched battle, there was a series of single combats and Béranger was restored to power. Not long afterwards, Gui died in A.D. 894.

Guibert: From Andernas. Youngest brother of William.

Guiélin: A nephew of William, brother of Bertrand and the son of Bernard of Brabant.

Haton: One of the Twelve Peers.

Hermeniart: Also Ermengard or Hermengard of Pavia. Wife of Aimeri of Narbonne, and mother of William.

Herod: Several rulers bore this name in Jewish history. It was probably Herod the Great who ruled when Jesus was born, and he is the one associated with the murder of the Holy Innocents. (See Matthew 2:16–18.) Herod the Great died ca. 4 B.C. His son is known as Herod Antipas, and he ruled Galilee. It was under his reign that John the Baptist was put to death, after Salome's famous dance. See Matthew 14:3–12 and Mark 6:17–29.

Hungier: A free burgher of Tours.

Innocents: The young children slaughtered by King Herod in Jerusalem; he sought to slay the future "king of the Jews." See Matthew 2:16.

Jerusalem: An ancient city in Palestine (modern-day West Bank), where Jesus was executed. In medieval times (ca. 1030), Jerusalem had a large population of traders from Amalfi who had built a church, a monastery and a hospice for travelers and pilgrims. When the Seljuk Turks gained control of Palestine, they severely persecuted the Christians and burnt many of the churches. It was news of these outrages that led to the Council of Clairmont in 1095 and brought about the first Crusade in 1099. Subsequently, the Latin Kingdom of Jerusalem was established in 1099, which was later destroyed by Saladin in 1187. The Latin Kingdom was moved and re-established at Saint-Jean-d'Acre; it lasted until 1291.

Jonah: An Old Testament prophet who survived three days and nights in the belly of a sea creature, commonly held to be a whale. See Jonah 1:17 and Matthew 12:40.

Joyous: The name of William's sword given to him by Charlemagne, whose own sword was also named "Joyous." Naming swords was an ancient Germanic tradition.

Judas (Iscariot): One of the twelve disciples of Jesus, who betrayed him for thirty pieces of silver. See Matthew 26:14.

Julian: Lord of the city of St. Giles.

Julius Caesar: Consul and dictator of Rome (100–44 B.C.), but in *The Crowning* he is a pagan ruler and forefather of King Galafrez.

Laon: Ancient cathedral city northwest of Rheims and northeast of Paris. Saint Rémi instituted a bishopric in the city (in the 5th century A.D.), and it served as a major cultural and intellectual center well into the Renaissance. It was also a stronghold of Carolingian kings in the 10th century. Hugh Capet, after becoming king in A.D. 987, moved the seat of kingship to Paris.

Lombardy: A region in northern Italy bordering Switzerland in the north. The name derives from the Langobards (Longbeards), a Germanic tribe from Jutland that overran this area in A.D. 568, under their leader Alboin. The Langobards reached the height of their power in the 7th and the 8th centuries, during which time they ruled much of Italy from the north to the south. When they began to threaten Rome, Pope Stephen II appealed to Pepin the Short (Charlemagne's father), who came to Italy and saved the Papal lands. When the Langobards again threatened Rome in 772, Charlemagne intervened and defeated the Langobards completely. Then, he had himself crowned (in 774) as King of the Langobards, with their iron crown (a Langobard emblem of royalty). A remnant of the Longobard kingdom (the Duchy of Benevento) was captured by the Normans in the 11th century. The only legacy of the Langobards was the name of the region where they once ruled. Paul the Deacon recorded the history of the Langobards.

Longinus: Also, Longeus. The traditional name of the (blind) Roman soldier who pierced Christ's side with his spear. He smeared Christ's blood on his eyes and immediately regained his sight, and was converted. He bears traces of the Germanic god Höder.

Loth (Saint): The Old Testament patriarch and nephew of Abraham, who lived in the city of Sodom, and whose wife turned into a pillar of salt. See Genesis 11:27.

Louis I or the Pious: (A.D. 778–840). Son and successor of Charlemagne, crowned Emperor of the Holy Roman Empire at Aix-la-Chapelle (Aachen) in A.D. 813, four months before the death of his father. He ruled over the undivided empire until his death in A.D. 840.

Lyons: Name of a forest that surrounded Lyons-la-Forêt, around the River Eure, east of Rouen.

Magdalen (Saint Mary): Her name either means that she was from Magdala, on the west coast of the Sea of Galilee, or perhaps it means "curly haired" in Hebrew; curled hair was a sign of an adulteress. The New Testament mentions perhaps three persons who can be identified as the Magdalen. One is the sinful woman (Luke 7:36–50). One is the woman who accompanied Jesus (Luke 8:2–3), who had seven demons cast out of her (Mark 16:9), who stood at the foot of the cross (Mark 15:40; Matthew 27:56; Luke 23:49), and who laid Jesus in his tomb and witnessed the resurrection (Mark 16:4 and 9; Luke 24:2; John 20:1–2 and 11–16). The third possibility is the sister of Martha and Lazarus (Luke 10:38–42; John 11). According to French tradition, Mary Magdalen, together with Lazarus and some companions, came to Marseilles and converted Provence; some thirty years later she died at Aix-en-Provence and was buried at the oratory of St. Maximin. The chronicler Sigebert tells us that her relics were removed to Vézelay in A.D. 745 through fear of the Moors. The Church of La Sainte-Baume now houses these relics.

Manessier: Called "the Youth." One of the Twelve Peers, but not according to *The Song of Roland*.

Martin of Tours (Saint): A.D. 316–400. Bishop of Tours. The cathedral where he was buried became an important pilgrimage site in the Middle Ages.

Mary (Saint): The mother of Jesus. According to the *Commemoratorium de Casis Dei*, addressed to Charlemagne, Mary died in Jerusalem and was buried on Mount Olivet where a church marks the spot (probably the Church of the Assumption).

Mecca: Birthplace of Mohammad, in Saudi Arabia. It is a revered pilgrimage site for Muslims.

Methuselah: An Old Testament patriarch who is said to have lived 969 years. See Genesis 5:27.

Mohammad: (A.D. 570–632). The prophet of Islam, but in the *chansons de geste*, he is a god of the pagans and the Saracens.

Montjeu: This is the ancient Alpine pass route (between Canton Valais and the Valle d'Aosta) that leads into northern Italy, now known as Grand-Saint-Bernard, in Switzerland. It has been in use since the Bronze Age (ca. 800 B.C.), and was also used by Hannibal in 217 B.C. The Roman Emperor Augustus built a temple to Jupiter and gave the area its name in antiquity and the early Middle Ages – Mons Iovis or Mont Jeu, that is "the Mountain of Jupiter." In A.D. 800 Charlemagne crossed Montjeu before and after his coronation in Milan. In the early 900s Huns and Saracens swept through the region, wreaking great destruction, and soon thereafter they set themselves up as the guardians of the Montjeu pass. They were eventually ousted by King Canute of Norway and King Rudolf III of Burgundy. Soon after, Bernard of Menthon, the bishop of Aosta (later Saint Bernard), established a hospice for travelers coming down the pass.

Montjoie: The war-cry of the French in the Middle Ages. It is also perhaps the name of Charlemagne's banner. Montjoie is often used in conjunction with Saint Dénis. There are several interpretations as to the meaning of *montjoie*. Some believe that it comes from *Mons Iovis* (the hill of Jupiter or Jove), for in Roman times, a battle was often directed from a high place referred to as *Mons Iovis*. From there, it became an expression that meant, "Hurrah!" or "Praise be!" Some suggest that it refers to Mont Gaudi where Charlemagne received his banner. And some believe that it derives from the Frankish term *mund-gewi* ("holder of the land"), referring to the saint or king as the protector of the land.

Montpellier: An ancient city in the Languedoc-Roussillon region. In the 8th century the region was greatly devastated by the on-going battle between Charles Martel and the Saracens. During the 9th–10th centuries, Montpellier became an important financial center, with thriving banks and extensive trade in precious metals, especially gold. Montpellier also minted coins, which could be used in the trade between the Christian north and the Moorish south. For example, Bishop Béranger de Frédol struck the "Miliarensis" coin that bore the name "Mohammad" on it; it was struck for use in the Mediterranean, an area long held by the Muslims. Montpellier remained an important financial center until the Renaissance.

Montrueil: Montrueil-sur-Mer ("By the Sea") in Pas-de-Calais. It had an important cloth market in the Middle Ages.

Mont-Saint-Michel: Fortified island on the border of Normandy and Brittany, where an abbey was built by Bishop Aubert of Avranches in A.D. 706. It was dedicated to the Archangel Saint Michael, since legend has it that he directed the Bishop to build a shrine to him. In A.D. 966, the earlier abbey was taken over by the Benedictines, who greatly encouraged the cult of Saint Michael and made the island an important pilgrimage site. By the time of William the Conqueror, the abbey had many royal benefactors.

Moses: Hebrew prophet and lawgiver, who led the Israelites out of Egypt. See Exodus 2 and 12.

Narbonne: The city of Aimeri, William's father. Narbonne is the major town of the Aude *department*. It was the capital of the Roman *Provincia Narbonensis* and later part of the Carolingian *Septimania*. Narbonne was conquered by the Visigoths in A.D. 413. The Franks referred to the area as *Gothia*. In A.D. 719, the Arabs captured Narbonne; forty years later, they were driven out by Pepin the Short (Charlemagne's father).

Navarre: Both Spain and France now share the territory once called Navarre. Spanish Navarre lies partly in the mountainous region of the Pyrenees and partly on the banks of the Ebro River. Navarre (or Vasconia) was never completely conquered by anyone, although the Romans, the Carolingians and the Moors did hold the area for brief periods of time. Charlemagne captured Pamplona in A.D. 778, the same year he was defeated by the Navarese and the Basques at the Pass of Roncesvalles. By A.D. 852, Navarre had its own kingship under Semen Garcia. The dynasty lasted up to 1076 when Alfonso VI, the King of Castile, and Sancho Ramirez together ruled Navarre.

Nero: A.D. 37–68. Roman Emperor, but in the Middle Ages considered a ruler in Hell, therefore a devil.

Nero's Field: The medieval *pratum Neronis*, near St. Peter's Basilica, where stood the gardens of Nero, as well as the *Circum Neronis*, where St. Peter was martyred according to Christian tradition.

Nicodemus: An important figure in Jerusalem who became a follower of Jesus and donated a tomb for Christ's burial. See John 3:1.

Noah: An Old Testament patriarch and grandson of Methuselah. The story of Noah is related in Genesis 5–9. When God decided to destroy humankind, He saved Noah, because he was righteous, along with his family and a male and female from all the living species, and placed them all in an ark. After the Flood, the surviving humans and the various creatures repopulated the earth.

Norman: An inhabitant of Normandy, of Viking descent.

Normandy: The Frankish district of Neustria, which was permanently settled by Viking raiders, led by Rollo, in the 9th–10th centuries.

Olivier: Or Oliver. One of the Twelve Peers and a companion of Roland; killed with him at Roncesvalles.

Orable: A Saracen queen, daughter of King Desramed, and wife of Tibalt of Africa. She lived in Orange and helped William conquer the city. Afterward, she received baptism and was renamed Guibourg, and then married William.

Orange: An ancient Roman city near the Rhône River, north of Avignon. Orange is not mentioned in *The Crowning*.

Orléans: The ancient capital of the Duchy of Orléans in the Loire valley. It was considered a royal city, and became part of the Capetian Duchy of France. In Charlemagne's time, Orléans was an important university town, specializing in classical literature.

Paris: Main seat of King Louis and the capital of the kingdom of France. The city was named after the Celtic tribe (the Parisii) that lived in the area. It was Clovis (the Merovingian king) who came to Paris and made it his capital in A.D. 497. This tradition continued under the Carolingians, the Capetians, the Valois, and the Bourbons. In A.D. 845 and 850, the Vikings sacked Paris, but the worst attack took place in 885; the siege lasted a year, and only ended when the Emperor Charles the Fat paid the Vikings a ransom and allowed them to use the Seine to carry on raids in Burgundy.

Paul (Saint): Born Saul in Tarsus, he came from a strict Jewish family (II Timothy

1:3). He was an early persecutor of Christians until his conversion on the road to Damascus (Acts 9:1–19), at which time he took on the name "Paul." He was martyred in Rome during the reign of Nero, probably ca. A.D. 67. Tradition states that he died the same day as St. Peter.

Peter (Saint): Originally named Simon and born in Bethsaida, near Lake Genesareth. He is considered to be the first among the twelve disciples of Jesus. He died during the Neronian persecution of Christians in Rome in A.D. 67.

Pierelage: The seat of Dagobert of Carthage and conquered by William. Probably Peralada in Gerona (Catalonia).

Poitiers: The ancient capital of the medieval county of Poitou. It was a great religious center and the seat of Visigothic kings. The Franks captured Poitiers in A.D. 507, led by Clovis. In A.D. 732, Charles Martel (the grandfather of Charlemagne) beat back the Saracens (led by Abd-er-Rahman) at the Battle of Poitiers (fought somewhere between Poitiers and Tours). Poitiers was often raided by Vikings, who had settled in Normandy. In 1152, it came under English rule (which lasted until 1372).

Poitou: A county established in the 8th century that stretched from the Atlantic east to the Vienne River. It was the personal fief of Charlemagne.

Pope: The Bishop of Rome and head of the Roman Church; also known as the Apostle of Rome, in that he represents St. Peter. The title "pope" was first used to designate the Roman Pontiff in the 4th–5th centuries by Pope Siricius (died A.D. 398) and Ennodius of Pavia (died A.D. 473). In earlier periods, "pope" meant any priest. It was Gregory VII (?1020 – 1085) who finally reserved the title for the Roman Pontiff.

Red Sea: Perhaps the Gulf of Suez. The Hebrew name is *Yam-Suph*, which perhaps means the "Sea of Reeds." The name "Red Sea" is just as uncertain, although the term is a direct translation of the Greek *eruthra thalassa* ("red sea") and the Latin *Mare Rubrum*; but we cannot know why it was so called. Be that as it may, the Red Sea is famous in Judeo-Christian belief in that this was where Moses parted the waters and led the Israelites out of Egypt; the waters then closed upon the Egyptians, killing them all. The story is told in the Old Testament (Exodus 14 and 15).

Richard (of Rouen): Also called "Richard the Old" and "Richard the Red." Duke of Normandy and father of Acelin. He is maimed by William and eventually thrown into a dungeon in Paris, where he dies. There is no known duke of Normandy by this name during the time of Charlemagne; however, in the *chansons de geste*, the dukes of Normandy are often named Richard. Nevertheless, there is a residue of history in the story of Richard of Rouen. After William Longsword was assassinated in A.D. 943, King Louis IV of France, feigning friendship, took Richard, the young son of William, under his protection and brought him to Laon, where he threw the young duke into prison. But within a few days Richard escaped and returned to Normandy. Thereupon, the Normans lured Louis IV to Rouen, where they slaughtered his retinue and in turn threw him into prison. Much later, Louis was handed over to Hugues le Grand, Count of Paris and Duke of France.

Thus, Richard the young Duke of Normandy had his revenge. Perhaps it is this "treason" that is recalled in *The Crowning*.

Roland: The hero of the epic poem *The Song of Roland*. There may have been earlier "Roland" songs since Wace tells us that Taillefer sang of Roland's deeds before the Battle of Hastings (in 1066), to stir the men. Roland (or Hrodland) was Charlemagne's warden of the Breton March and was killed in a pass in the Pyrenees when the Navarese and the Basques cut off the rear guard of the Frankish army in A.D. 778. Legend has it that Roland was Charlemagne's nephew and one of the Twelve Peers.

Romany: The ancient province of Italy whose capital was Ravenna, ruled by the Goths. In Carolingian times, Romany was part of the Papal State and Charlemagne's empire.

Rome: The ancient city that lies on the banks of the Tiber and is the Apostolic See of St. Peter and of the Popes. It was also the second capital of Charlemagne's empire (the first being Aix-la-Chapelle).

Romulus: The legendary founder of Rome, who along with his brother Remus was raised by a she-wolf. In *The Crowning* he is a "fuzzy" pagan lord of Rome, through whom the Saracen claim ownership of the city.

Rouen: Capital of the Duchy of Normandy. The city has been continuously inhabited since 56 B.C. (and probably earlier) and was important in Celtic and Roman times. After the Viking conquest and settlement ca. A.D. 840, Rouen became the capital of the new Duchy of Normandy, created from the Carolingian district of Neustria.

Russia: The kingdom of the Slavs. The name "Russia" derives from the "Russ" (the name of the Vikings, or Varangians, who invaded the area under their leader Rurik, who established the city of Novgorod ca. A.D. 862). Viking rule opened Russia to Western Europe, and trade between the two began in earnest. In *The Crowning* Russia is considered the spawning ground of savage pagans.

St. Denis: Royal abbey on the outskirts of Paris; also the burial place of the French kings.

St. Giles: Modern-day Saint-Gilles-du-Gard on the Rhône delta. It was a famous place of pilgrimage in the Middle Ages, where the relics of Saint Giles were housed. Saint Giles, who flourished in the later half of the 7th century and the early part of the 8th, was renowned for his piety. He is often represented with a hind.

Saracen: A generic term for Muslims in the Middle Ages. Originally, the term referred specifically to the Arabs living in Syria, but with the expanding Muslim incursions into Europe, the term "Saracen" took on a wider meaning to include all the peoples who were not Christian and who came from the East.

Savaris: A nephew of William.

Seier of Plessis: A knight in William's army. Plessis is a common (generic) place-name used to designate a knight of little importance.

GLOSSARY

Simeon (Saint): The ascetic St. Simeon Stylites, who died in A.D. 591. His method of meditation was to climb a pillar and do penance for months or years on end.

Simon Magus: Simon the Magician. He was an early Christian convert who sought to buy the gift of the Holy Ghost. See Acts 8:9ff.

Simon the Leper: An early follower of Jesus in Bethany. See Matthew 26:6 and Mark 14:3).

Spain: The term *Espaigne* denotes Spain, but often meant all the lands held by the Moors of Spain, which in the 8th and 9th centuries included much of Southern France.

Spoleto: Once the capital of the dukes of Lombardy from A.D. 568, Spoleto was annexed into the Carolingian Empire in A.D. 774 and was made a Duchy or Margravate. After the demise of the Carolingians, it became part of the Papal States, although in the 11th century it fell into the hands of the Normans. From 1139 onward, it reverted to Papal hands, until Napoleon took it in 1806.

Tenebrez: A Saracen king. His name means "darkness."

Three Kings: The three magi or wise men (identified as "kings" in the Middle Ages), who came to pay homage to the baby Jesus. See Matthew 2.

Tiber: The river that flows through Rome and empties into the Tyrrhenian Sea.

Toulouse: Situated on the Garonne River, Toulouse was part of Roman Gaul, and from A.D. 419 it served as the capital city of the Visigoths. In A.D. 508, Clovis and his Franks captured the city; and by 781, it had become the capital of Aquitaine. It gained independence from Carolingian rule in 843 and was ruled by its own counts. Toulouse was the cultural and literary center of medieval Europe. By the late 12th century, the dukes of Toulouse effectively ruled the entire Languedoc region. Their suzerainty ended during the Albigensian Crusades (1208–1229), and Toulouse became the possession of the French crown.

Tours: An ancient cathedral city on the Loire River, which was a center of Christian learning under Gregory of Tours and Alcuin. Tours was an ancient Gallo-Roman town that grew rapidly after the death of its first bishop Saint Martin. In A.D. 732, near Tours, Charles Martel halted the Moorish invasion of Europe. Tours was ruled by the counts of Blois and Anjou.

Tudèle: Or Tudela. A city on the Ebro River in Navarra, Spain. Tudela flourished under the Moors and was an important cultural and literary center, especially for Jewish thought. It produced such outstanding Jewish thinkers as Benjamin of Tudela (died in 1173), Aben Ezra (1089–1164), and Judah Halevy (1075–1141).

Turk: In the Middle Ages, Turks were separated from the Saracens by way of origin. While the Saracens were the Moors of Spain, Turks were the nomads that had begun to impinge upon Byzantine territories in Asia Minor in the 11th century, and had begun to seriously harass pilgrims going to the Holy Land and destroyed many churches and monasteries (a situation which led to the First Crusade). The tribe that expanded into Christian territory was the Selkuj Turks, who under their leaders Tughril and Alp Arslan posed a great threat to Christendom in the east, and paved the way for the eventual collapse of the Byzantine Empire.

Tuscany: A region in north central Italy bordering on the Tyrrhenian Sea. Florence is the capital of this province. From the 6th to the 8th centuries A.D., it was a Lombard duchy; later it became a Carolingian March up to the 12th century. Tuscany's last Frankish ruler, Matilda (who died in 1115), gave the province into papal hands. Notable schools of art developed in this region from the 11th century onwards.

Twelve Peers: Or Paladins. A band of warriors that accompanied Charlemagne. The origins of this practice are rooted in the Germanic *comitatus* (a retinue of noble warriors who served a lord). The names of the Twelve Peers are: Roland, Olivier, Turpin, Naimes, Guillaume of Toulouse, Davelon de Roucesvalles, Baudoin, Archbishop of Rheims, Bishop of Laon, Bishop of Challon-sur-Marne, Bishop of Beauvais, Bishop of Langres, Bishop of Noyon, Duke of Bavardia. This list is not canonical and most epics mention many other Peers.

Virgin (the): Also, the Blessed Virgin. See **Mary (Saint)**.

William: The hero of the "William of Orange Cycle" of verse epics (which total 24 *chansons de geste*). He is the son of Aimeri and Hermeniart of Narbonne, and is one of seven brothers. His sister Blanchefleur marries King Louis. He is nicknamed "Shortnose" and "Strongarm."

Yves: One of the Twelve Peers in *The Song of Roland*.

Yvoire: Companion of Yves and also one of the Twelve Peers.

Bibliography

Editions

W.J.A. Jonckbloet, ed. *Guillaume d'Orange, chansons de geste des XIe et XIIe siècles.* The Hague, 1854–1864.

Ernest Langlois, ed. *Le couronnement de Louis.* Paris: Firmin Didot, S.A.T.F., 1888.

_____, ed. *Le couronnement de Louis. Chanson de geste du XIIe siècle.* Paris: Champion, 1921.

Translations

Joan M. Ferrante, trans. *Guillaume d'Orange. Four Twelfth-Century Epics.* New York and London: Columbia University Press, 1974.

Glanville Price, et al., trans. *William, Count of Orange: Four Old French Epics.* London: Dent, 1975.

General

Elizabeth Aubrey. *The Music of the Troubadours.* Bloomington: Indiana University Press, 1996.

Dominique Boutet. *La chanson de geste: forme et signification d'une écriture du moyen age.* Paris: Presses Universitaires de France, 1993.

Peter Damian-Grint. *The New Historians of the Twelfth-Century Renaissance: Inventing Vernacular Authority.* Suffolk; Rochester, NY: Boydell Press, 1999.

Norman Daniel. *Heroes and Saracens.* Edinburgh: Edinburgh University Press, 1984.

Wolfgang van Emden, Philip E. Bennett, Alexander Kerr, eds. *Guillaume d'Orange and the Chanson de geste: Essays Presented to Duncan MacMillan.* Reading: Société Rencesvals (British Branch), 1984.

Ursula Ernst. *Studien zur altfranzösischen Verslegende (10–13. Jahrhundert): die Legende im Spannungsfeld von Chanson de geste und Roman.* Frankfurt am Main; New York: P. Lang, 1989.

Edmond Faral. *Les jongleurs en France au moyen age.* Paris: H. Champion, 1964.

Valérie Galent-Fasseur. *L'épopée des pèlerins: motifs eschatologiques et mutations de la chanson de geste.* Paris: Presses Universitaires de France, 1997.

Edward A. Heinemann. *L'art métrique de la chanson de geste: essai sur la musicalité du récit.* Geneva: Librairie Droz, 1993.

A. Hindley and B. Levy. *The Old French Epic: An Introduction.* Louvain: Peeters, 1953.

Sarah Kay. *The Chanson de geste in the Age of Romance.* Oxford: Clarendon Press, 1995.

Jean-Pierre Martin. *Les motifs dans la chanson de geste: définition et utilization.* Discours de l'epopée médievale, I. Lille: Centre d'Études Médievales et Dialectales, Université de Lille, 1992.

Claude Riot. *Chants et instruments: trouvères et jongleurs au moyen age.* Paris: R.E.P.A.R.T., 1995.

François Suard. *La chanson de geste.* Paris: Presses Universitaires de France, 1993.

_____. *La chanson de geste: écriture, intertextualités, translations.* Paris: Centre des Sciences et de la Littérature, Université de Paris, 1994.

_____. *Chanson de geste et tradition épique en France au moyen age.* Caen: Paradigme, 1994.

R.N. Swanson. *The Twelfth-Century Renaissance.* Manchester; New York: Manchester University Press, 1999.

Jeremy Yudkin. *Music in Medieval Europe.* Englewood Cliffs, NJ: Prentice-Hall, 1989.

Index

Aachen 86, 101, 108
Aachener Dom 101
Abd-er-Rahman 111
Abderraman ibn Mavia 8
Abel 34, 101, 103
Abelard, Peter 2
Aben Ezra 113
Abila 101
Abilant 80, 101
Abraham 94, 108
Acelin 62, 63, 64, 65, 66, 97, 98, 101, 111
Acquae Silviae 95
Acts of Saint Peter 95
Adam 34, 41, 92, 101, 103, 105
Africa 96
Agobard 102
agon 5
Aiane 8
Aimeri 20, 30, 37, 54, 55, 81, 82, 84, 101, 103, 106, 114
Aimers 37, 93, 101
Aix-en-Provence 108
Aix-la-Chapelle 3, 6, 16, 86, 101, 108, 112
Al Andalus 86
Alban Hills 96
Albigensian Crusade 113
Alboin 107
alcorbitanas 8
alcubes 75, 99
Alcuin 88, 113
Alelme 101
alétheia 4, 13
Alfonso VI 110
Alfonso the Warrior 102

Aliaume 62, 63, 64, 101
Alicante 99
Alion 32, 47, 70, 72, 81, 84, 101
Aller 88
Alori 54, 101
Alp Arslan 114
Alsace 106
Amalfi 90, 107
Amarmonde 68, 101
Amiens 2
Anastasia, St. 34, 92, 101
Andernas 37, 101, 106
Andorra 102
Angelier 30, 102
Anglo-Saxon 86
Anjou 14, 15, 88, 102, 113
Annadore 69, 102
Anseune 101, 105
Antioch 95
Antwerp 103
Aosta 109
Aquinas, Thomas 2
Aquitaine 6, 8, 14, 103, 105, 106, 113
Arabia 77, 102, 108
Arabs 8, 24, 82, 93, 99, 109
Aragon 42, 62, 95, 102
Aramaic 94
Ark 34
Arnéïs d'Orléans 4, 18, 19, 102
Arthur 98, 102
Astronomus 13
Athens 94
Attigny 7
Aubert 109
Aude 109

Augustine, St. 13
Augustus 108
Avalon 62, 63, 98, 102
Avallon 98, 102
Aventine 96
Avignon 110
Avranches 104, 109

Babylon 105
Bakhtin, Mikhail 5, 13
Baldur 93
Balkans 91
Balshazzar 95, 105
Baratron 41, 94, 102
Barcelona 87
Basque 87, 110, 112
Bavaria 6, 15, 86, 102
Bayeux Tapestry 92
Beauce 104
Beauvais 2
Becket, Thomas 2, 14
Beelzebub 41, 94, 102
Belgium 103
Benedict, St. 8
Benevento 86, 107
Benjamin, Walter 13
Benjamin of Tudela 113
Berber 104
Béranger 30, 103, 106
Bérenger de Fredol 109
Bernard 8, 37
Bernard, St. 10, 11, 14, 20, 56, 101, 103, 106
Bernard of Menthon 109
Berry 45, 103
Bertrada 104
Bertrand 8, 18, 23, 25, 26, 45, 46, 47, 54, 56, 57, 58, 65, 66, 73, 74, 76, 79, 80, 81, 84, 85, 90, 95, 103, 106
Bethlehem 34, 103
bezant 98, 99
Béziers 105
Blanchefleur 99, 103, 114
Blois 93, 113
Bohemia 86
Bois-le-Duc 103
Bonaventura 2
Boniface, St. 102
Bordeaux 6, 68, 87, 101, 103, 106
Bourges 103
Bovon 37, 101, 103
Brabant 20, 37, 101, 103, 106

Brahant 75, 99
Bresle 88
Breton March 87, 111
Brie 53, 103
Brittany 15, 69, 88, 103, 108
Bruttium 103
Burgundian Code 87
Burgundy 93, 98, 102, 109, 110

caduceus 97
Caelian 96
Caesar, Julius 28, 108
Cahut 32, 47, 92, 103
Cain 34, 101, 103
Calabria 38, 103
Calvary 35, 103
cannibalism 91, 92
Canute of Norway 109
Capella Palatina 86, 101
Capitoline 96
Capua 23, 24, 104, 105
Carolingian 6, 86, 87, 98, 99, 102, 103, 107, 109, 110, 112, 113, 114
Cartagena 91, 104
Carthage 28, 69, 91, 104
Castellar 99
Castile 110
Catalonia 105, 106, 111
Cathars 91
centrifugal 5, 9
centripetal 5
Champagne 103
Champion 50, 104
chanson de geste 1, 2, 3, 12, 96, 103, 108, 111
chaos 3, 4, 5, 9
Charlemagne 2, 3, 6, 8, 15, 19, 20, 21, 22, 24, 25, 38, 52, 53, 61, 78, 81, 86, 87, 88, 89, 94, 101, 102, 103, 104, 105, 106, 107, 108, 109, 110, 111, 112, 114
Charles II 6, 7
Charles Martel 109, 111, 113
Charles the Bald 103, 104
Charles the Fat 110
Charles the Simple 89
Chartres 2, 78, 104
Chasseneuil 6
Cherbourg 104
chiasmus 4
Childeric III 87
Chronicon Moissiacense 8, 14
Ciquaire 23, 104

INDEX 119

Clairvaux 10
Clement of Alexandria 92
Clinevant 84, 104
Clovis 110, 111, 113
Cluny 8
Colmar 7
Comarchis 37, 101, 103, 104
comitatus 114
Commercy 104
Constance, Lake 106
Constantine 99, 103
constellation 6
Cordova 86
Corsica 86
Corsolt 3, 9, 10, 23, 29, 31, 32, 38, 42, 43, 46, 82, 84, 90, 91, 92, 93, 94, 96, 99, 101, 104
Cotentin 69, 104
Council of Clairmont 107
Cremuz 23, 104
The Crowning of Louis 1, 2, 3, 4, 5, 6, 7, 8, 9, 10, 11, 87, 91, 94, 98, 99, 105, 107, 110, 111, 112

Dagobert 105
Dagobert of Carthage 69, 105
Damascus 95
Daniel 42, 95
Darius 105
Dark Ages 2
David 91
denier 20, 41, 64, 77, 87, 88
Denis, St. 2, 30, 48, 53, 58, 61, 66, 82, 84, 105, 113
Denmark 86, 88
Desramed 96, 110
Devil 29, 30, 33, 35, 85, 92, 93, 102, 105
Dido 91
Dijle 103
Diocletian 92, 101
dualism 2, 91
Dumézil, Georges 14

Ebro 87, 105, 109, 113
Egypt 90, 111
Elbe 105
Eleanor of Aquitaine 13, 14
emir 23, 44, 52, 74, 87, 90
England 86
Ennodius of Pavia 111
Ensérune 105

epic 1, 2, 4, 5, 6, 9, 11
Eresburg 88
Ermengard 8, 37, 106
Ermoldus Nigellus 8
Ernaut 37, 105
Esquiline 96
Estolt de Langres 30, 105
Eure 104, 108
Europe 10
Eve 34, 41, 92, 101, 103, 105
exemplum 4

Flanders 91
fragment 6, 9
France 3, 8, 11, 12, 14, 15, 16, 20, 21, 25, 51, 53, 54, 55, 63, 69, 70, 78, 79, 80, 85, 86, 87, 88, 93, 103, 105, 106, 109, 110, 111
François I 103
Franks 18, 20, 31, 32, 33, 36, 37, 38, 44, 45, 76, 85, 88, 102, 104, 105, 113
Friuli 106
Fulbert 104

Gabriel 26, 27, 105
Gaeta 90
Galafrez 3, 23, 25, 27, 28, 30, 31, 46, 47, 50, 52, 74, 91, 96, 99, 104, 105, 107
Galilee 106, 108
Garin 37, 101, 105
Garonne 113
Gascon 102
gastald 104
Gaul 105, 113
Guatier, Abbot 67, 105
Guatier, Clerk 59, 105
Gautier de l'Hum 30
Gautier of Toulouse 45, 47, 49, 59, 65, 84, 105
Gautier of Tudèle 57
Gellone 8
Gembloers 103
Gérin 30, 105
Gerona 105, 106, 111
Gibraltar 104
Gironde 17, 37, 68, 87, 105, 106
gleeman 12
Gnosticism 95
Golden Gates 35, 92, 106
Golgotha 103
Goliath 91
Gothic 2
Goths 112

Grandoyne 103
Grand-Saint-Bernard 108
Gregory VII 111
Gregory of Tours 113
Guaifier 23, 25, 48, 51, 74, 76, 96, 104, 106
Gualdin 54, 106
Guarin of Rome 58
Gui of Germany 4, 74, 76, 77, 78, 79, 80, 81, 82, 83, 84, 99, 104, 105
Guibert 37, 101, 106
Guibourg 96, 110
Guiélin 23, 26, 45, 47, 49, 81, 84, 103, 106

Hague Fragment 8, 14
Hannibal 91, 108
Haton 30, 106
Hebrew 94, 95, 108, 109, 111
Heidegger, Martin 13
Helena 104
Henry (II) of Anjou 14
Henry of Lausanne 91
Hérault 105
hermeneutics 10, 11, 13
Hermengard 106
Hermeniart 37, 101, 106, 114
Hernant li Roux 101
Herod 34, 92, 106
heteroglossia 5
historia rerum gestarum 2, 3
history 2, 3, 4, 5, 9, 11, 13
Höder 93, 107
Holy Innocents 34, 92, 106
Homer 97
Hrolf 88
Hugh Capet 107
Hugues le Grand 111
Hungary 97
Hungier 65, 106
Huns 108

ideology 9
Ile-de-France 1, 12, 103, 105
In honorem Hludovici 8
In Praise of the New Knighthood 10
India 99
Indo-European 14, 90
Ingelheim 7
Irminsul 88
Isidore of Seville 94
Islam 93, 108
Italy 103, 104, 106, 107, 108, 112

Jabal Tarik 104
Jerome, St. 103
Jerusalem 5, 35, 90, 93, 96, 103, 104, 106, 107, 108, 110
Jesus 10, 18, 31, 47, 69, 93, 95, 99, 103, 105, 106, 107, 108, 110, 111, 113
Jews 35, 37, 41, 90, 92, 93, 104, 106
John the Baptist 106
Jonah 95, 107
jongleur 1, 12
Joseph of Arimathea 35
Joyous 83, 84, 89, 95, 107
Judah Halevy 113
Judas 35, 41, 107
Julian 69, 98, 107
Julian, St. 8
Jupiter 108, 109
Justinian I 103
Jutland 107

laisse 1, 3, 92
Landulf I 104
Languedoc 101, 113
Languedoc-Rousillion 109
langue d'oïl 11, 12
Laon 86, 99, 107, 111, 114
Lebanon 101
Le Mans 88
Leo III 89
Lévi-Strauss, Claude 96
Llobregat 87
Loire 102, 110, 113
Lombard 104, 114
Lombardy 15, 107, 113
Longinus 35, 42, 93, 107
Longobards 107
Loth (Lot) 40, 94, 108
Lothair I 6, 7, 106
Louis II 106
Louis IV 111
Louis VI (Louis the Fat) 2, 3, 6, 7, 13, 86, 87, 98
Louis VII 2, 3, 7, 13
Louis the German 6, 7
Louis the Pious 3, 4, 5, 6, 7, 8, 9, 11, 12, 13, 16, 17, 18, 19, 20, 21, 24, 25, 44, 45, 52, 53, 54, 55, 59, 60, 61, 62, 63, 64, 66, 67, 68, 69, 74, 75, 76, 77, 78, 79, 80, 83, 84, 85, 86, 88, 89, 90, 97, 98, 99, 102, 103, 104, 108, 114
Louvain 103
Low Countries 103

INDEX

Lügenfeld 7
Lyons 70, 102, 108

Magnus, Albertus 2
Mahomet 10
Mainz 106
Manessier 30, 108
mangon 98
Marseille 108
Martin of Tours, St. 53, 54, 59, 97, 105, 108, 113
Mary, St. 20, 33, 34, 36, 43, 55, 83, 104, 105, 108, 114
Mary Magdalene 35, 93, 108, 110
Mathfrid 102
Matilda 114
Maximin, St. 108
Mecca 37, 108
Merovingian 87, 105
Methusaleh 35, 93, 108, 110
Meuse 104
Michael, St. 109
Milan 108
Mohammad 32, 33, 36, 37, 38, 39, 40, 47, 49, 50, 92, 93, 103, 108, 109
Monte Talfo 96
Montjeu 22, 23, 53, 75, 108, 109
Montjoie 66, 77, 84, 109
Montpellier 45, 46, 73, 96, 97, 109
Montreuil 85, 109
Mont-Saint-Michel 69, 109
Moors 8, 87, 101, 102, 108, 110, 113
Moravia 86
Moses 42, 90, 109, 111
motet 2
Murcia 104

Naples 86, 90, 103, 104
Narbonne 20, 56, 81, 82, 101, 103, 106, 109, 114
Navarre 15, 109, 110
Nebi-Abil 101
Nebuchadnezzar 105
Nero 41, 42, 62, 81, 94, 95, 110, 111
Neustria 104, 110, 112
Nicodemus 35, 110
Nijvel 103
Noah 34, 110
Nominoë 103
Normandy 14, 15, 89, 101, 104, 109, 110, 111, 112
Normans 8, 21, 88, 103, 107, 110, 113

Norway 108
Nota Emilianense 8, 14
Notre Dame Cathedral 2

Oder 86
Odo, Bishop 92
Ogier the Dane 105
Old French 2, 11, 12, 103, 104
Old High German 12
Olivier 30, 110, 114
Orable 53, 96, 110
Orange 96, 110, 114
Orbien 8
Orderic Vitalis 8, 14
Oriflamme 105
Origen 95
Orkney 88
Orleans 74, 102, 110
Ostia 90
Otto of Germany 106

Paderborn 89
pagans 3, 4, 5, 17, 25, 26, 30, 31, 33, 36, 37, 38, 39, 40, 43, 44, 47, 49, 89, 91, 92, 93, 96, 107, 108, 112
Paladin 79, 103, 114
Palatine 96, 107
Pamplona 87, 110
Pannonia 86, 97
Paris 2, 12, 59, 78, 82, 85, 86, 99, 103, 104, 105, 107, 110, 111, 112, 113
Passover 93
Paul, St. 42, 90, 94, 95, 110, 111
Paul the Deacon 107
Pavia 106, 111
Peace of God 98
Pepin I 6, 7
Pepin the Short 101, 104, 107, 109
Perlada 105, 111
Peter, St. 20, 22, 26, 27, 29, 30, 31, 38, 40, 42, 44, 46, 47, 87, 89, 90, 91, 94, 95, 96, 110, 111, 112
Philip Augustus 93
Philippe 13
Picardy 1, 12, 88
Pierelarge 68, 111
Pierre de Bruys 91
Poitiers 59, 67, 68, 111
Poitou 68, 69, 111
Pope 9, 11, 24, 25, 26, 27, 28, 30, 31, 38, 39, 43, 44, 45, 48, 49, 50, 51, 52, 53, 74, 87, 91, 92, 94, 95, 111

Provence 108
Pseudo-Clemtines 95
Puys d'Olivesa 102
Pyrenees 87, 102, 109, 112

Quirinal 96

Ramiro 102
Ravenna 112
Red Sea 23, 90, 111
Rémi, St. 107
Remus 112
res gestae 2, 3
Rheims 2, 102, 107
Rhône 110, 113
Richard of Rouen 4, 14, 52, 53, 55, 56, 65, 66, 67, 69, 70, 71, 72, 73, 74, 98, 101, 111
Robert 89
Robert Guiscard 103
Roderic 104
Rognvald 88
Roland 30, 87, 98, 112, 114
Rollo 88, 89, 104, 110
Rome 5, 9, 16, 20, 22, 23, 27, 28, 29, 30, 38, 39, 40, 43, 45, 46, 47, 50, 53, 58, 74, 75, 76, 78, 80, 82, 83, 84, 85, 89, 90, 91, 92, 93, 94, 95, 96, 104, 107, 111, 112, 113
Romany 23, 38, 112
Romulus 28, 112
Roncesvalles 87, 110
Rouen 2, 14, 52, 53, 69, 101, 108, 111, 112
Rudolf III 109
Rurik 112
Russia 23, 89, 112

's-Hertogenbosch 103
Sabine 96
Saint-Giles 69, 98, 107, 112
Saint-Gilles-du-Gard 112
Saint-Jean-d'Acre 107
Saint-Malo 88
Sainte-Baume 108
Saladin 107
Salerno 106
Salic Code 87
Salome 106
Sancho Ramirez 110
Santa Camisia 104
Santiago de Compostela 8, 9

Saracens 3, 4, 5, 8, 9, 10, 11, 14, 15, 23, 24, 28, 36, 37, 38, 39, 40, 42, 44, 45, 48, 49, 90, 91, 93, 94, 96, 102, 103, 104, 105, 106, 108, 109, 111, 112, 113
Sardinia 86
Sargossa 8, 87, 88, 102
Satan 91, 94
Saul 110
Savaris 54, 112
Saxons 88
Saxony 86
Scandinavia 86
Schelde 103
Second Crusade 13
Seier of Plessis 59, 112
Seine 88, 105, 110
Semen Garcia 110
Sicily 86, 103
Sigebert 108
Sigismund 93
Simeon, St. 42, 95, 113
Simon Magus 42, 95, 113
Simon the Leper 35, 41, 113
Siricius 111
Sodom 94, 108
Soissons 99
Solomon 90
Song of Roland 2, 12, 98, 102, 103, 105, 108, 112, 114
Spain 8, 75, 90, 91, 93, 99, 102, 109, 113
Spanish March 86, 87
Spoleto 74, 106, 113
Suger, Bishop 3, 7, 13, 98, 105
Swinthila 104
Syria 95, 112

Taillefer 112
Tanchelm 91
Tarik 104
Tarsus 110
Tassilo 102
teleology 4
Templars 10
Tenebrez 23, 113
Tertullian 95
Thegan 13
theocentric 3
Theodebald 18
Theodosius 95
Tibalt 96, 110
Tiber 48, 49, 84, 90, 99, 112, 113

Tivoli 96
Toulouse 8, 47, 113
Tours 55, 71, 97, 106, 108, 111, 113
Traité d'Union Perpetuelle 103
translation 11
Tre Fontane 95
trope 4, 5, 13
tropology 4, 13
Troubadours 12
Truce of God 98
Tudèle 57, 113
Tughril 114
Turks 30, 36, 43, 44, 45, 107, 113
Turpin, Archbishop 30, 102, 114
Tuscany 15, 38, 114
Twelfth Century Renaissance 2, 12
Twelve Peers 8, 30, 102, 103, 105, 106, 108, 110, 112, 114

Uccle-Brussels 103
Umbrian 96

Valais 108
Valence 99
Valerian 92, 101
Valle d'Aosta 108
Varangian 112
Vasconia 109
Vatican 106
Verden 88
Verdun 104
Vézelay 108
Vienne 111
Viking 88, 89, 104, 110, 111, 112

Viminal 96
Visigoths 93, 104, 109, 111, 113
Vita domni Willelmi Abbatis 8, 14

Wace 112
Wala 102
warden 18, 20, 26, 87, 89, 112
warrior ethic 3, 9–10, 11, 14
Widukind 88
William I 8
William VI 8
William VIII 9
William IX 8, 14
William Fièrebrace 9
William Longsword 89, 111
William of Conches 94
William of Montreuil 8
William of Orange 2, 3, 5, 7, 8, 9, 10, 11, 15, 18, 19, 20, 21, 22, 23, 24, 25, 26, 30, 31, 33, 36, 37, 38, 39, 40, 41, 42, 43, 44, 45, 46, 47, 48, 49, 50, 51, 52, 53, 54, 55, 56, 57, 58, 59, 60, 61, 62, 63, 64, 65, 66, 67, 68, 69, 70, 71, 72, 73, 74, 75, 76, 77, 79, 80, 81, 82, 83, 84, 85, 86, 89, 90, 92, 93, 94, 95, 96, 97, 98, 99, 101, 103, 104, 105, 106, 107, 109, 110, 111, 112, 114
William of Toulouse, St. 8
William the Conqueror 89, 92, 109
wolfhound 23, 89, 90

Yonne 98, 102
Yves 30, 114
Yvoire 30, 114